GW00456571

Astrology

for Beginners

Stars Hold the Key of Your Life Path

GIOVANNI
DA RUPECISA

TEMPLUM DIANAE MEDIA

2023 - All Rights Reserved

Before you continue reading, the author and publisher explicitly request that you read and understand the legal notes to clarify some basic aspects of the relationship between the parties.

Legal notice:

this book is subject to exclusive copyright; reading it is intended for personal use only. Please also note that you are not permitted to modify or use any of the sections of this book at all, either for free or for a fee; you are absolutely not permitted to use, quote from, or paraphrase any section or sections of this book or its contents without the written and signed consent of the author and/or publisher.

Legal notice about the author's and publisher's disclaimer:

The author and publisher affirm and reiterate that all information contained in this work, taken individually or in its entirety, depending on the sensibilities of the individual reader or reader, may have an educational-educational purpose or that of mere pastime.

The author and publisher of this volume, while reminding all readers that no warranty of any kind is explicitly or implicitly given, affirm and reiterate that all the information contained in this work, being derived from critical reading of various sources, possesses the highest degree of accuracy, reliability, topicality and completeness in relation to their ability to research, synthesize, process and organize the information.

Readers are aware that the author is in no way obligated to provide any kind of legal, financial, medical, or professional assistance or advice, and indeed recommends that they, before attempting any of the techniques or actions set forth in this book, contact a professional legally licensed to practice, as per current legislation.

By reading this introduction, each reader agrees, explicitly or implicitly, that in no event shall the author and/or publisher be liable for any loss, direct or indirect, resulting from the use of the information contained in this book, including but not limited to errors, omissions, or inaccuracies.

www.templumdianae.co

İNDEX

Table of Contents

**Teaching Materials
included**

Scan this code to get
your Video Course included in the book, an introduction to the
world of the occult and the paranormal

Or follow this link:

https://templumdianae.co/the-witchy-course/

This Material will give you access to Exclusive training materials
to improve in your path !

İNTRODUCTİON

Dear seekers of spiritual enlightenment,

Life is a journey filled with twists and turns, moments of joy and sorrow, victories and defeats. Yet, amidst the chaos and unpredictability, there's a desire that pulses within each of us — a desire to uncover the hidden threads that connect our experiences, to decipher the enigmatic map of our life's path. Welcome to "Astrology for Beginners: Stars Hold the Key of Your Life Path," a guide tailored to those who seek clarity, guidance, and empowerment in the cosmic dance of existence.

Are you feeling lost in the labyrinth of your life, unsure of which path to tread?

Do relationships, careers, or financial struggles seem to overshadow your journey?

If you're grappling with these questions, you're not alone. Countless individuals experience moments of doubt and confusion, yearning for direction and solace. The weight of stress and overwhelm can become suffocating, leaving us gasping for insight to light our way. And yet, skepticism may hold us back, leaving us yearning for something we can trust—something that resonates with our innermost being.

In the shadows of our fears, we find ourselves haunted by the specters of wrong choices, loneliness, failure, and the vast unknown. The stigma attached to our interests, like astrology, might cast doubt upon our pursuit of self-discovery. The fear of being deceived by charlatans lurking in the realms of the mystical can cripple our desire to seek answers. But know this: your fears are shared, and they can be overcome.

Embedded within us are dreams of purpose, deeper relationships, career triumphs, financial security, and, above all, happiness. We long for tools to unveil our true potential, to make decisions with conviction, to steer the wheel of our destiny, and to embrace the connection between our individual selves and the cosmic forces that surround us.

Allow me to share a personal story that brought me to this exploration of astrology's profound influence. In the depths of my own spiritual and esoteric quests for self-development, I stumbled upon a revelation that would change the course of my life. In my pursuit to combat the suffocating grip of anxiety and depression, I unearthed a treasure trove of ancient wisdom that spanned across cultures, religions, and eras—astrology, the common thread that wove the tapestry of humanity's spiritual evolution.

As I delved into the realms of esoteric knowledge, I discovered that astrology was not just a distant science of distant stars; it was the cornerstone of many mystical practices. From alchemy to numerology, from ancient cults to modern magick, the influence of the celestial bodies resonated through time. My journey into these mysterious domains offered me a lifeline—a lifeline that would help me navigate the storms that raged within and without.

My odyssey into the mystical realm of esoteric knowledge revealed that astrology transcended its status as a mere science. From the enigmatic art of alchemy to the mystical language of numerology, and even to the hallowed rituals of ancient cults the influence of celestial bodies reverberated resolutely through the annals of time. It was as if the cosmos itself was etching its indelible mark upon our human narrative.

A decade-long expedition unfolded as I immersed myself in the depths of astrology's intricate tapestry. I traversed the celestial realms, decoding the language of planets, houses, and aspects. Yet, as I embarked on my journey, I faced a formidable challenge — there existed a scarcity of practical guides that distilled the intricate nuances of astrology into digestible wisdom. The intricate web of information often led to confusion rather than enlightenment. This scarcity ignited a resolve within me — an unwavering determination to chart my own course, to transcribe my personal notes and insights, and to create a handbook that would serve as a guiding light for those who, like me, grappled with life's uncertainties.

And thus, "Astrology for Beginners: Stars Hold the Key of Your Life Path," was born. Within its pages, I've meticulously transcribed the learnings garnered over years of dedicated study, transforming my personal notes into a beacon of clarity and understanding. This handbook stands as a testament to my commitment to aiding those who face similar struggles, offering insights that speak directly to the pain points, fears, and desires that guide our human experience.

As we traverse the following chapters, you'll find a compendium of knowledge carefully assembled over years of dedicated study and exploration. This handbook is designed to be the guide I wish I had when embarking on my astrological journey—a guide that distills complex concepts into practical insights and actionable wisdom. By sharing my journey and the fruits of my labor, I hope to offer solace, direction, and empowerment to those who yearn for a deeper connection with their life's purpose and the cosmos that envelops us.

In "Astrology for Beginners," we embark on a shared quest—a journey that unveils the cosmic map and offers tools to understand the intricate design of our lives. As we traverse the pages ahead, we'll explore the fundamental principles of astrology, demystify its language, and empower you to harness its wisdom for your growth.

Whether you're new to the world of astrology or already have a flicker of interest, this book is tailored to meet you where you are. We'll address your pain points, confront your fears, and fan the flames of your desires. The celestial bodies have stories to tell—stories that resonate with your own. Together, we'll unlock the secrets they hold and illuminate the path to self-discovery, healing, and transformation.

So, if you're ready to unravel the tapestry of your existence, to grasp the guiding thread that links your past, present, and future, then turn the page and embark on this cosmic journey. The stars have aligned to bring you here, and together, we'll find the light that leads the way.

WITH LOVE AND LIGHT.

CHAPTER 1
A LIFE WITHOUT ASTROLOGY

İN A WORLD BURSTİNG WİTH İNFORMATİON AND

CHOİCES, it's easy to question whether delving into the depths of astrology is really worth your time and energy. Why should you bother unraveling the mysteries of the cosmos when there are so many other pursuits clamoring for your attention? In this chapter, we explore the concept of "A Life Without Astrology" and shed light on the challenges and missed opportunities that may arise if you decide to forego this ancient and illuminating practice.

Imagine embarking on a journey without a map or compass, unaware of your strengths, weaknesses, and unique qualities. A life without astrology is like navigating uncharted waters blindfolded. Astrology provides a profound mirror to your inner self, helping you understand your motivations, desires, and potential. Without this tool, you may miss the opportunity to truly know yourself.

Relationships form the backbone of human existence, yet without astrology, they often remain enigmatic puzzles. A life without astrology means relying solely on chance when it comes to partnerships, friendships, and romantic connections. You might find yourself repeatedly drawn to incompatible people or struggle to understand the dynamics of your relationships.

Choosing a career path can be one of life's most daunting challenges. Without astrology, you might find yourself drifting from one job to another, unsure of your true calling. Astrology can offer valuable insights into your vocational strengths and passions, guiding you toward a fulfilling and purpose-driven career.

Personal growth and self-improvement are pursuits that enrich our lives and lead to a deeper sense of fulfillment. A life without astrology may mean missing the transformative potential that celestial insights can offer. Astrology can illuminate the areas where you can grow, helping you evolve into the best version of yourself.

Life is filled with challenges and uncertainties, from health issues to financial setbacks. Astrology provides a unique perspective on these challenges, offering guidance on how to navigate them and uncover hidden opportunities for growth and healing. Without astrology, you may feel more vulnerable and ill-equipped to face life's inevitable ups and downs.

Astrology invites you to reconnect with the cosmos and recognize your place in the grand tapestry of the universe. A life without astrology may lead to a sense of disconnection from the natural world and the celestial rhythms that influence our lives. Embracing astrology can rekindle this profound connection and provide a sense of purpose and meaning.

Navigating Life's Uncharted Waters

In a world that moves at an increasingly rapid pace, the quest for self-discovery often takes a backseat to the demands of daily life. Yet, the absence of self-knowledge can lead to a host of challenges and missed opportunities. Imagine for a moment that you've embarked on a journey—a journey through life—without the aid of a map or compass. You find yourself navigating uncharted waters, unsure of your direction and the obstacles that lie ahead. This, in essence, is what a life without astrology can feel like.

Astrology, often regarded as a mystical and ancient art, serves as a powerful tool for self-discovery. It's like a mirror that reflects the depths of your inner self, illuminating facets of your personality, motivations, desires, and potential that might otherwise remain shrouded in darkness.

The Labyrinth of Self

Without astrology, you might be wandering through the labyrinth of your own psyche, bumping into walls and missing hidden passages. You may have a vague sense of your strengths, weaknesses, and unique qualities, but these remain elusive and undefined. The intricate web of your personality, intricately woven with cosmic threads, is left unexamined.

Astrology's gift lies in its ability to decode the celestial influences that shape your character and life path. It reveals the cosmic forces at play during your birth, offering insights into your inherent tendencies and the guiding principles of your existence. Your motivations, desires, and even your hidden aspirations come into focus under the astrological lens.

For instance, you may discover that your fiery Aries sun sign infuses you with a relentless drive for achievement and leadership. Or, your Piscean moon sign might unveil a deep well of empathy and creativity that you've often struggled to express.

Perhaps the most profound aspect of self-knowledge through astrology is the unveiling of your potential. It's like discovering a hidden treasure trove within yourself. You may learn that your Capricorn rising sign bestows you with remarkable discipline and a strong work ethic. Armed with this knowledge, you can channel these qualities toward ambitious goals and aspirations, ultimately reaching new heights in your life.

In the absence of astrology, your self-awareness might remain limited to surface-level observations. You may make choices and decisions without fully understanding why you're drawn to certain paths or experiences. Relationships, career choices, and life's many crossroads become murkier to navigate, often leading to feelings of confusion and dissatisfaction.

Astrology, however, offers a beacon of clarity. It allows you to step out from behind the blindfold, to gain a more profound understanding of your true self. Armed with this knowledge, you can chart a course through life's unpredictable waters with confidence and purpose.

As we journey through the pages of this book, we'll delve deeper into the world of astrology and unveil the myriad ways it can enrich your life. While a life without astrology is certainly possible, it may come at the cost of self-discovery, meaningful relationships, and personal growth. Join us on this exploration, and together we'll uncover the boundless potential that astrology holds for you.

CHAPTER 2
DON'T MİSS ANOTHER
DATE WİTH THE STARS

IN THE VAST TAPESTRY OF THE COSMOS, there exists a

profound and ancient wisdom known as astrology — a tool that
has the potential to guide us through life's tumultuous journey,
illuminating our path with the brilliance of the stars themselves.
Yet, despite the undeniable awareness of the transformative
power of astrology, many among us continue to stumble in the
dark, failing to harness its potential to alter the course of our
lives.

The paradox is that we are often well aware of how astrology
can positively impact our lives. We've heard tales of its
astonishing ability to foretell destiny, explain personality traits,
and even reveal hidden talents. We understand the potential it
holds to unlock the doors to a brighter future. We know that the
alignment of celestial bodies can, and does, influence our daily
existence. And yet, despite this awareness, we find ourselves
losing out on the profound benefits that astrology can bestow

Imagine having the keys to a treasure chest, a chest filled with
untold riches and opportunities, right in front of you. You
acknowledge their presence, but for some inexplicable reason,
you choose not to unlock the lid. The result? A double failure.
First, the failure to recognize the invaluable resource at your
disposal, and second, the failure to act upon it.

Here lies the intriguing paradox: the universe, which is infinitely
generous and boundlessly compassionate, responds differently
to those who possess the solutions to their life's challenges but
refuse to utilize them. It's almost as if the cosmos becomes a
stern judge, ready to penalize and punish more severely those
who possess the keys to transformation yet choose to keep them

locked away, denying themselves and others the opportunity for growth, success, and fulfillment.

The Double Failure: The Treasure Unclaimed

Picture this: before you lies a treasure chest, not just any chest, but one brimming with boundless riches and countless opportunities. The lid of this chest is adorned with the most intricate lock, and you hold the key in your hands. You know it's there, the treasure chest, and you know the key can unlock its bounty. Yet, inexplicably, you choose to let it sit there, undisturbed and unopened.

The outcome of this decision is a double failure. Firstly, it's the failure to recognize the immeasurable resource that lies at your fingertips, a resource that could potentially transform your life. It's like standing before a towering tree laden with ripe, succulent fruits and not reaching out to pluck a single one.

Secondly, it's the failure to act upon the knowledge, the failure to grasp the opportunity, to turn the key and unlock the chest of possibilities. It's akin to having a map to undiscovered lands and opting to stay in familiar territory, never venturing beyond the horizon.

Now, here's where the cosmic paradox deepens. The universe, in all its grandeur and magnanimity, seems to have a unique response to those who possess the solutions to their life's challenges but consciously choose not to utilize them. It's almost as if the cosmos assumes the role of a stern, impartial judge, ready to render its verdict.

In this cosmic courtroom, those who hold the keys to transformation but leave them untouched face a different kind of penalty. The universe appears to scrutinize them more closely, and its judgment carries a weightier consequence. It's as though the cosmos gently admonishes, "You've been given the means to not only better your own life but also to positively impact others' journeys. To deny this, is to deny growth, success, and fulfillment for yourself and those around you."

In the pages that follow, we'll delve deeper into the mysteries of astrology, exploring how this ancient art can reshape our lives, illuminate our paths, and guide us toward the success we crave. We'll uncover the secrets of tapping into the universe's abundant wisdom and examine the consequences of letting this opportunity slip through our fingers.

We'll delve into the consequences of not seizing the opportunity, and we'll learn how, together, we can harness the universe's abundant wisdom. Remember, dear reader, you hold the power to change your destiny, to shape your future, and to unlock the life you've always dreamed of. The universe beckons; are you ready to answer its call?

So, dear reader, as we embark on this cosmic journey together, remember that you hold the power to change your destiny, to shape your future, and to seize the life you've always dreamed of. The universe is ready to share its secrets; are you ready to embrace them?

CHAPTER 3
BECOME A STARCHILD
UNLOCK YOUR INNER
POWER

W E GLİMPSED THE PROFOUND İMPACT THAT

ASTROLOGY CAN HAVE ON OUR UNDERSTANDİNG of ourselves and the world around us. Now, we embark on a journey of empowerment, a transformational path that astrology can illuminate. As you dive into the rich tapestry of astrological wisdom, you'll discover the keys to unlock your inner power and embrace the radiant "starchild" within you.

At birth, each of us is imprinted with a cosmic blueprint — a unique configuration of celestial energies that shape our character and life's trajectory. This celestial map is intricately designed, much like a fingerprint, and it holds the key to unlocking your inner potential. Astrology enables you to decipher this cosmic code, revealing the starry influences that guide your journey on Earth.

Progressions offer a fascinating perspective on your life's unfolding narrative. They symbolize the gradual evolution of your inner self and reflect the changing seasons of your life. Understanding progressions allows you to embrace personal growth consciously.

As you delve deeper into astrology's vast universe, you'll realize that it's not merely a tool for self-discovery but a cosmic counselor within you. It serves as a trusted advisor, offering profound insights into your relationships, career, and life purpose.

The Starchild's Radiant Awakening

In the heart of every human being, there exists a dormant celestial force, the "starchild." This radiant essence is a reflection of the cosmic energies that danced in the heavens at the moment of your birth. It holds the secrets of your true self, your purpose, and your untapped potential. As we delve deeper into the profound world of astrology, you'll begin to feel this inner starlight flicker to life.

strology serves as a cosmic mirror, reflecting the brilliance of your unique soul. With each astrological insight, a piece of this mirror is polished, allowing you to see yourself more clearly. You'll recognize your strengths, talents, and challenges as they are written in the stars. Through this recognition, you become the master of your own destiny.

ife, like the universe, is in constant motion. Astrology equips you with the tools to navigate these cosmic currents. Imagine sailing on a ship with no knowledge of the winds or the stars to guide you. Astrology becomes your compass, helping you harness the power of celestial influences.

When you encounter challenges, astrology offers solace and direction. It whispers that cosmic storms, like earthly ones, shall pass. It assures you that during the darkest nights, a North Star shines brightly, guiding you towards your true purpose. By embracing astrology, you gain the wisdom to set your sails, allowing the winds of fate to carry you toward your desired destination.

Life is an intricate tapestry woven with choices. Some decisions may seem insignificant, while others alter the course of your existence. Astrology empowers you to make choices that resonate with your soul's purpose. It whispers guidance in moments of doubt and reinforces your intuition.

With the cosmic insights gained through astrology, you'll embark on a journey of informed choices. When standing at life's crossroads, you'll possess the wisdom to decipher which path aligns with your highest self. Your choices become a tapestry of stardust, weaving your unique story into the cosmos.

Self-discovery is a lifelong odyssey, and astrology is your steadfast companion on this quest. As you unlock the secrets of your Sun, Moon, and Ascendant signs, you'll uncover layers of your being previously concealed. The radiance of your "starchild" begins to shine through, illuminating the darkest corners of your psyche.

With each revelation, you'll embrace both your light and your shadow. You'll dance with the contradictions and complexities that make you whole. Astrology reminds you that you are a microcosm of the universe—a symphony of planets and stars. Through self-discovery, you become the conductor of this cosmic orchestra, harmonizing your existence with the celestial rhythms.

Astrology is not a mystical prediction of an unchangeable fate; it's a guide for your journey of empowerment. It encourages you to seize the reins of your life and become the master of your cosmic destiny. As the "starchild" within awakens, you'll tap into reservoirs of resilience, creativity, and wisdom.

With astrology as your ally, you'll march boldly into the world, aware of your unique gifts and purpose. You'll navigate the complexities of human existence with grace, compassion, and authenticity. Your radiant essence will inspire others to embark on their own cosmic journeys, creating a tapestry of interconnected souls.

As we venture deeper into the realm of astrology, you'll unlock the cosmic wisdom that lies dormant within you. The "starchild" within—the radiant essence of your true self—awakens to its full potential. By embracing the insights and guidance that astrology offers, you'll navigate life's challenges with grace, make informed choices, and embark on a transformative journey toward self-discovery and empowerment. Together, we'll illuminate the path to becoming the master of your cosmic destiny

CHAPTER 4
SO, YOU WANT KNOW THE STARS?

T HE NİGHT SKY HAS ALWAYS HELD AN ALLURE

THAT TRANSCENDS TİME AND CULTURE.

Gazing up at the vast expanse of stars, humanity has sought meaning, guidance, and a connection to something larger than ourselves. This innate curiosity about the cosmos is what has led many of us to embark on a journey into the world of astrology — a journey that unravels the mysteries of the universe and sheds light on our own lives.

At its core, astrology is the art of deciphering the cosmic code — reading the language of the planets, stars, and their positions at the time of our birth to gain insights into our personalities, relationships, and life events. It's as if the universe itself is whispering secrets about our destinies, waiting for us to listen.

The roots of astrology stretch back to ancient civilizations that looked to the heavens for guidance. From the ancient Babylonians to the sophisticated astrological systems of India and China, cultures across the globe recognized the profound influence of celestial bodies on earthly affairs. This journey through time reveals astrology's enduring significance in shaping human beliefs, cultures, and philosophies.

Astrology operates on a complex system of symbols, each carrying its own unique meaning. Planets are the actors, signs are the costumes they wear, and houses are the stages on which their dramas unfold. Understanding this celestial alphabet is essential for interpreting the birth chart — a personalized snapshot of the cosmos at the moment you entered this world.

Imagine the birth chart as a cosmic blueprint—an intricate map of your life's journey. Every planet and point occupies a specific place in one of the twelve houses, each house representing a different facet of your life. Unraveling this map offers a glimpse into your personality, relationships, career path, and more.

As planets journey through the sky, they form angles, or aspects, with one another. These interactions create a dynamic interplay of energies, influencing your experiences and choices. Some aspects promote harmony, while others provoke challenges. Learning to read these conversations unveils the intricate dance of your life's narrative.

So, you want to know the stars? Welcome to the world of astrology—a realm where the mysteries of the cosmos intertwine with the story of your life. As you delve deeper into this journey, you'll discover how the stars' positions at your birth reflect the essence of your being. It's a journey that requires curiosity, patience, and an open heart—a journey that has the power to illuminate your path and unveil the key to unlocking your true self.

As we venture into the following chapters, you'll explore the intricacies of the zodiac signs, the cosmic houses, and the multifaceted language of astrology. By the time you've navigated this celestial landscape, you'll be well-equipped to interpret your birth chart, gain insights into your life's purpose, and forge a profound connection with the stars that have watched over you since your first breath.

the Essence of Astrology

At its very essence, astrology unfolds as a tapestry woven from the threads of the cosmos—a cosmic language that speaks to us through the planets, stars, and their celestial choreography. It beckons us to unravel the intricate patterns etched across the skies and interpret the messages they carry. Imagine astrology as a celestial symphony, with each planetary movement and alignment composing a melody that resonates through the very fabric of our existence.

In its essence, astrology is a bridge between the macrocosm and the microcosm, inviting us to explore the interplay between the vast universe and the individual soul. At the moment of our birth, the positions of the planets and stars imprint a unique energetic signature upon us. This imprint, captured within our birth chart, becomes a roadmap that guides us through the labyrinthine corridors of our lives.

Astrology becomes a powerful tool, akin to a metaphysical decoder, allowing us to decipher the cosmic code that holds sway over our destiny. It unveils a profound truth: that the universe is not a detached entity, but rather an interconnected web where every entity, from the tiniest atom to the grandest galaxy, dances in harmony. Our lives, too, are a part of this cosmic ballet, choreographed by the celestial energies that imbue our birth chart.

Picture the birth chart as a celestial canvas, painted with the hues of the planets and signs. Each planet symbolizes a unique facet of our being, and the signs in which they reside infuse these facets with distinctive qualities. The cosmic houses then become the stages on which these planetary actors perform, each house representing a specific arena of our life's drama. The interplay of planets, signs, and houses tells a story — a story of strengths and challenges, aspirations and fears, victories and setbacks.

As we delve into the study of astrology, we embark on a journey to unearth the treasures hidden within this cosmic language. It's akin to deciphering an age-old manuscript that has traveled through time, inscribed with the wisdom of the ages. Astrology invites us to connect with the wisdom of our ancestors, who gazed at the same constellations and planets with awe and reverence, seeking guidance in their celestial dance.

In this quest for understanding, astrology extends an invitation — an invitation to listen to the universe's secrets, whispered through the language of the stars. It beckons us to embark on a voyage of self-discovery, illuminating the depths of our personalities, our potentials, and the challenges that shape us. Like a gentle breeze carrying echoes from distant galaxies, astrology whispers insights about our relationships, career paths, and life's turning points.

Astrology, at its very core, stands as a testament to the interconnectedness of all things. It's a reminder that we are not isolated beings, but integral components of a larger cosmic design. Through its lens, we can perceive the symphony of our lives — the harmonies and dissonances, the crescendos and pauses. With each birth chart we explore, we unlock a new verse in the ever-evolving song of the universe, gaining a deeper understanding of ourselves and our place within the grand cosmic narrative.

Cosmic pillars of divine science

As we delve deeper into the enigmatic world of astrology, we find ourselves standing at the crossroads of ancient wisdom and modern insight. The foundations of astrology are not mere theoretical constructs; they are the bedrock upon which the cosmic language is built. These foundations, like celestial constellations, guide us through the labyrinthine corridors of planetary energies, signs, and houses.

At the heart of astrology lies a profound symbology — a language woven from planets, signs, and houses. Each symbol carries within it layers of meaning, a cosmic lexicon that can be deciphered with precision. Just as a painter's brushstroke creates a masterpiece, the positioning of a planet in a sign and house crafts a celestial portrait unique to each individual. Understanding this celestial alphabet is the key to unlocking the cosmic message contained within the birth chart.

The planets — those luminous wanderers of the night sky — assume the roles of celestial actors in astrology's grand stage. Each planet embodies a unique archetype, an energetic force that colors the canvas of our lives. From the assertive vitality of Mars to the harmonizing influence of Venus, each planet contributes to the intricate symphony that shapes our personalities, desires, and experiences.

As the planets don their zodiacal attire, they take the stage within the houses — a dynamic setting where life's narratives unfold. Each house represents a distinct arena of experience, from the self-discovery of the First House to the transformational depths of the Eighth House. The houses create a canvas on which the planetary actors dance, depicting the themes and challenges that color our individual journeys.

In the cosmic realm of astrology, aspects are the dialogues between planets — a symphony of energies that shapes our lives. Whether in harmonious trine or challenging square, aspects reveal the interplay of planetary forces. The art of interpreting aspects unveils the melodies and tensions within our birth charts, offering insights into our strengths, challenges, and potential paths of growth.

To unlock astrology's secrets, we must grasp the notion of cosmic time and the creation of the birth chart. The moment of our birth — a unique collision of planetary positions — leaves an indelible mark upon our souls. Understanding the birth chart's creation process gives us the tools to interpret its messages, as if we are reading a diary written by the universe itself.

As we immerse ourselves in these foundational principles, we prepare ourselves for a journey of exploration and self-discovery. Each symbol, planet, sign, and house we encounter is a treasure chest waiting to be opened — a portal to insights that can shape our understanding of ourselves, our relationships, and the universe that cradles us. Embrace these pillars of cosmic wisdom, for they are the lanterns that illuminate the path of astrological understanding ahead.

Ancient Pathways of Celestial Wisdom

The corridors of time lead us through a tapestry woven with threads of cosmic insight. Tracing the origins of astrology is akin to embarking on a journey across civilizations, cultures, and continents — a journey that unveils the universal fascination with the stars that has guided humanity's quest for understanding since time immemorial.

Ancient Babylon: The Cradle of Astrology
Gazing Skyward for Divination

In the heart of ancient Mesopotamia, the cradle of human civilization, the Babylonians gazed upon the night sky with a profound sense of wonder. They meticulously tracked the movements of celestial bodies, recognizing patterns and correlations between planetary positions and earthly events. To them, the stars were not mere celestial decorations, but rather omens — signs from the gods themselves, guiding their decisions and shaping their destinies. This astrological practice laid the very cornerstone upon which the edifice of astrological knowledge would be built.

Egyptian Mysticism: Celestial Alignments and Cosmic
Rulership - Stars as Guides to the Afterlife

In the heart of the Nile, the ancient Egyptians wove their own celestial narrative. Their pyramids and temples were aligned with the stars, creating a bridge between the terrestrial and the divine. The concept of cosmic rulership emerged, where each planet was associated with a deity who influenced events on Earth. The stars, like eternal beacons, guided souls through the labyrinth of the afterlife, offering them safe passage into the embrace of the gods.

India: The Vedic Cosmos and Cosmic Harmony
Astrology as an Integral Part of Life

On the Indian subcontinent, the ancient Vedic seers gazed into the heavens and recognized the cosmic dance of energies. Astrology, or "Jyotish" as it's known in Sanskrit, became an integral part of daily life. The Vedic system incorporated celestial wisdom into medicine, philosophy, and the arts. Birth charts were created not only for individuals but also for cities and nations, attesting to the belief that the cosmic energies interwove with every facet of existence.

China: The Celestial Mandate and Cosmic Balance
Harmony Between Earthly and Celestial Realms

In the Far East, the Chinese developed their own unique approach to astrology. The Mandate of Heaven, a concept that linked the legitimacy of rulers to celestial alignment, became a guiding principle in governance. The cosmic balance between yin and yang, sun and moon, found its reflection in the dualistic philosophy of Daoism. The heavens were seen as a mirror of earthly affairs, and the study of astrology was a pursuit that aimed to maintain equilibrium between the two realms.

The Greek Mysticism of Cosmic Understanding

As celestial bodies continue their ageless dance across the skies, so too does the intricate art of astrology evolve through the currents of time

The very term "astrology" bears witness to its origins in ancient Greece. Derived from the Greek words "astron" (star) and "logos" (study or discourse), astrology is a marriage of celestial observation and intellectual inquiry. The Greeks were captivated by the notion that the stars held keys to understanding earthly affairs — a belief rooted in the recognition of celestial patterns mirrored in human life...

...But the fusion of "astron" and "logos" encapsulated more than just a linguistic marriage; it marked the birth of an enduring pursuit — a quest to unveil the interconnectedness of the cosmos and human existence. This intertwining of the celestial and the intellectual became a hallmark of astrology, a bridge between the ethereal beauty of the stars and the probing inquiry of human minds.

Within the context of the ancient Greek world, astrology wasn't merely a set of calculations and predictions; it held profound spiritual significance. It functioned as a conduit — a sacred link connecting the realms of gods, mortals, and the underbelly of existence. The Greeks believed that the positions and movements of celestial bodies were messages from the divine, decipherable through the language of the stars.

The Greco-Etruscan approach to astrology wasn't just an intellectual exercise; it was a way of life, a means to commune with the divine forces that shaped their world. It provided solace in times of uncertainty, insight into life's challenges, and a glimpse into the cosmic symphony that resonated beyond the veil of mortal existence. Astrology was, for them, a sacred discourse — a dialogue between the heavens and the hearts of humanity, a bridge between the earthly and the divine, a testament to the eternal fascination with understanding the universe and our place within it.

Within this intricate dance of language and knowledge lies a deeper understanding of how astrology was embraced by the Etruscan people — a bridge uniting the divine, the mortal, and the enigmatic realm of death.

For the Etruscan civilization, the stars were more than celestial bodies — they were the handprints of the divine upon the canvas of existence. The Etruscans held a deep reverence for the cosmic realm, viewing it as a realm infused with messages from their gods. In their eyes, the stars were like radiant emissaries, carrying cosmic whispers that conveyed insights into the intricate tapestry of human lives and the broader fate of their society.

Astrology, for the Etruscans, was not just a tool; it was a sacred art, a gatekeeper to divine wisdom. It allowed them to engage in a dialogue with their deities — a discourse facilitated by the intricate celestial patterns. Through the observation of the heavens, the Etruscans sought to decipher the divine intentions and gain insights that guided their decisions, both on personal and societal levels.

The Etruscans believed that the stars held the keys to not only the present but also the afterlife — a realm shrouded in mystery and the unknown. Just as astrology connected them to the gods and the earthly realm, it also acted as a conduit to understand the passage of souls into the realm of death. The positions of the stars at the time of a person's passing were believed to influence their journey in the realm beyond, further highlighting astrology's role as a cosmic link that traversed the boundaries of life and death.

In the intricate tapestry of Etruscan spirituality, astrology was woven into the very fabric of their existence. It was a guiding light in times of uncertainty, a source of insight for making vital decisions, and a key to unlocking the enigmatic aspects of life and death. By studying the celestial alignments, the Etruscans sought to find meaning within the chaos of existence, to understand the purpose behind the events that unfolded in their lives, and to honor their connection to the divine forces that shaped their world.

In essence, astrology was a sacred thread that wove together the threads of the divine, the mortal, and the realm of death. It was a language that resonated across dimensions, enabling the Etruscan people to engage with the cosmos, communicate with their gods, and explore the mysteries that lay beyond the veil of human understanding. Through astrology, the Etruscans sought communion with the universe—a communion that transcended time, bridging the gaps between different realms of existence and revealing the intricate interconnectedness of all things

A Synthesis of Mathematics and Mysticism

The Pythagoreans, a mystical and philosophical society, played a pivotal role in shaping the evolution of astrology. Their fascination with numerical relationships and cosmic harmonies led to the integration of mathematics and cosmology. Pythagoras and his followers believed that the celestial bodies emitted unique vibrations, influencing the fabric of existence. This connection between numbers and stars was a precursor to the intricate mathematical calculations embedded within astrological practice.

Pythagoras, a luminary whose name resonates through the ages, stood at the forefront of this mystical brotherhood. He and his followers were captivated by the harmonious proportions that underpinned the universe's grand design. To them, numbers were not mere symbols but the very essence of reality — a key to unlocking the secrets of existence.

The Pythagoreans' journey into the realm of numerical mysticism extended to the heavens above. They posited that the celestial bodies — those radiant luminaries that graced the night sky — were not silent spectators but resonant instruments. Each planet, star, and celestial entity emitted its own unique vibration — a cosmic symphony that rippled through the fabric of reality itself.

This belief in the celestial vibrations laid the foundation for an intimate connection between numbers and stars. The Pythagoreans believed that the celestial melodies were mirrored in the numerical relationships they discerned on Earth. The harmony of the cosmos found its echo in the mathematical relationships they uncovered — a harmonious dialogue between the celestial realm and the world of numbers.

This profound insight marked a precursor to the intricate mathematical calculations that would become intrinsic to astrological practice. The Pythagoreans' fascination with cosmic harmonies became a beacon guiding the development of astrological techniques. The very birth of the birth chart, a personalized snapshot of celestial positions at the moment of birth, was intertwined with their belief in the resonance between numbers and stars.

Within the birth chart, the planets and their positions were akin to musical notes on a cosmic staff. Each placement, each aspect formed a celestial chord that resonated with the unique vibration of an individual's soul. The Pythagoreans' legacy echoed in the intricate calculations astrologers would employ, forging a connection between the planets' harmonious movements and the symphony of an individual's life.

The Pythagoreans' exploration of numbers and cosmic harmony was an endeavor that transcended the realms of philosophy and mathematics — it cast its influence upon astrology, imbuing it with a deeper layer of complexity. The intricate dance between numbers and stars, between celestial symphonies and terrestrial existence, became an integral facet of astrological interpretation.

As we trace the lineage of astrological knowledge, we find the fingerprints of the Pythagoreans imprinted upon its core. Their fascination with numerical relationships and cosmic vibrations set the stage for the integration of mathematics and cosmology, elevating astrology to a realm where the universe's grand symphony met the nuanced intricacies of human destinies. In the cosmic dance of numbers and stars, the Pythagoreans left a legacy — a legacy that resonates through the ages, a bridge that connects the ethereal with the earthly, and a testament to the profound interplay between celestial insights and human understanding.

Hellenistic Astrology: The Birth of the Birth Chart

In the ever-evolving mosaic of human exploration, the Hellenistic period emerged as a pivotal juncture in the evolution of astrology. It was during this epoch that a groundbreaking innovation took root—the birth chart, a celestial fingerprint that transformed the way astrologers perceived the interplay between the cosmos and human existence. This evolution marked the journey from the cosmic to the personal, from the universal to the intimately individual.

As the stars continued their eternal dance across the sky, astrologers of the Hellenistic era delved deeper into the intricacies of celestial observation. They recognized that the position of the planets at the moment of an individual's birth created a unique cosmic signature—a blueprint that mirrored the individual's essence and destiny. This realization ignited a revolutionary shift in astrological practice.

With deft precision, astrologers began constructing birth charts, also known as horoscopes. These intricate maps portrayed the positions of the planets within the zodiacal framework at the time of birth. Each planet's placement, each aspect between them, was akin to a note in a cosmic symphony—a symphony that resonated with the essence of the individual and the trajectory of their life journey.

The birth chart became a sacred text, a celestial diary of the soul's alignment with the universe. No longer were astrological insights confined to general predictions about collective events; they now offered highly personalized revelations about an individual's character, potentials, challenges, and life path. This evolution was a testament to the evolving relationship between humanity and the cosmos — a relationship that transcended the realm of mere astronomical observation.

Astrologers began to decipher the intricate language of the birth chart — a language woven from planetary positions, zodiacal signs, and the angles between them. The interplay of these cosmic components painted a vivid picture of the individual's psyche, aspirations, relationships, and the various chapters that would unfold in their earthly journey. The birth chart became a canvas on which the story of a life was written, a symphony where planetary movements composed the melodies of existence.

This shift from the macrocosmic to the microcosmic was revolutionary. It marked a departure from broad cosmic influences to the intimate intricacies of individual destinies. Astrology, once a tool primarily used for predictions about the collective, now held the power to offer insights that resonated deeply within the heart of each person.

The emergence of the birth chart as a central tool transformed astrology into a deeply personal and introspective art. It highlighted the interconnectedness between the celestial and the earthly, demonstrating that the patterns of the stars were intricately interwoven with the fabric of human life. The Hellenistic period's contribution to astrological evolution became a testament to the dynamic dialogue between the heavens and the human experience — a dialogue that continues to unfold, revealing the endless layers of meaning and connection that reside within the cosmic tapestry of existence.

As the Roman Empire expanded, it absorbed the intellectual treasures of conquered lands — including the cosmic insights of the Greeks. Greek philosophers like Plato and Aristotle laid the philosophical groundwork that would fuel the Roman scholars' thirst for knowledge. Figures like Claudius Ptolemy, through his work "Tetrabiblos," translated and synthesized Hellenistic astrological wisdom, shaping the foundations of astrological practice for centuries to come.

The Cosmic Convergence of Christianity

In the fertile soil of the Hellenistic era, a unique alchemy transpired — one that would give birth to a new spiritual movement that transcended the boundaries of time and space. The synthesis of Hellenistic astrology and spirituality, intertwined with the emerging tapestry of Roman culture, played an unsuspecting role in the creation of Christianity — an enigmatic cult that would reshape the course of history.

In the Roman world, the synthesis of astrology and spirituality found itself woven into the cultural fabric. The Romans, known for their syncretism — a penchant for merging diverse belief systems — embraced the interplay between the cosmic and the divine. The celestial narratives of planets and stars intertwined with their pantheon of gods, providing a bridge between the earthly and the ethereal.

The emergence of astrology as a tool for personal insight and spiritual growth was a precursor to the cultural currents that would ultimately shape the advent of Christianity. The belief in cosmic influences on human affairs, the personal quest for meaning, and the yearning to connect with the divine all played their part in preparing the psychological and cultural landscape for a profound transformation.

Amidst this cultural milieu, the birth of Christianity emerged — an unexpected convergence of spiritual yearning, cultural syncretism, and astrological insights. The four Gospels — Matthew, Mark, Luke, and John — were crafted with a subtlety that belied their true depth. Embedded within their narratives are echoes of ancient astrological and mystical concepts — a cryptic manuscript that holds the keys to ancient cosmic wisdom.

The symbolic parallels between Christ's life and the journey of the sun across the zodiacal wheel have not escaped the eyes of astrological scholars. The narrative of Christ's birth, death, and resurrection mirrors the cycles of celestial bodies — a metaphorical reflection of cosmic truths. The esoteric significance of numbers and their ties to planetary archetypes subtly weaves a tapestry of astrological insight within the Gospel texts.

The synthesis of Hellenistic astrology, spirituality, and Roman culture cast a profound influence on the birth of Christianity. This enigmatic new cult, born from the convergence of ancient wisdom and celestial insights, would go on to shape the spiritual fabric of the Western world.

In the four Gospels, cosmic secrets are encrypted — a legacy of an era when celestial wisdom was interwoven with spiritual teachings. As humanity journeyed through the pages of history, these hidden connections served as a reminder that the threads of the cosmos are woven into the very essence of our existence. The synthesis of Hellenistic astrology and spirituality, culminating in the cosmic currents that birthed Christianity, speaks to the enduring dialogue between the heavens and the human heart — a dialogue that continues to resonate through the ages.

As the celestial clock continued its inexorable march, the dawning of the year 0 marked a pivotal turning point — a convergence of cosmic cycles and spiritual narratives that would forever alter the course of human history. This epochal juncture,

symbolized by the birth of Christ and the advent of Christianity,
ushered in the Age of Pisces — a new era that carried profound
astrological and symbolic implications.

In the grand symphony of the Precession of the Equinoxes — a
phenomenon caused by Earth's gradual wobble on its axis — the
stars seem to shift over time, giving birth to successive
astrological ages. The Age of Pisces, a period lasting
approximately 2,000 years, followed the Age of Aries and
preceded the Age of Aquarius. These astrological ages mirror the
zodiacal constellations they are named after, each carrying its
own unique energies and symbolism.

The transition from the Age of Aries to the Age of Pisces was
marked by a gradual shift of the vernal equinox point from the
constellation Aries to Pisces. This epochal shift, magnificently
timed with the birth of Christ, mirrored the thematic essence of
Pisces — a sign symbolized by the Fish. This astrological era
resonated with the spiritual narrative that Christ would later
embody.

Throughout the New Testament, Christ's interactions with
fishermen serve as parables that reflect his role as the Fisher of
Souls. In the Age of Pisces, Christ's message encapsulated the
essence of the Fish — the call to cast aside the material nets that
bind us to the worldly and embrace the divine call of the spirit.

The Piscean era, characterized by its sensitivity, empathy, and
connection to the mystical, found its embodiment in Christ — a
figure who preached love and redemption, who performed
miracles and embraced the downtrodden. Christ's miraculous
feeding of the multitude with fish and loaves, and the
symbolism of the Last Supper with bread and wine, further
intertwined the Piscean theme of sacrifice and spiritual
sustenance.

STARS HOLD THE KEY OF YOUR LIFE PATH

The Age of Pisces, with its inherent cosmic energies, served as a backdrop for the emergence of Christianity and the teachings of Christ. This era carried the resonance of the Fish — the spiritual and symbolic representation of Christ's mission to awaken humanity to a deeper, compassionate, and unified consciousness.

As the vernal equinox shifted into Pisces and Christ's presence graced the world, the threads of the cosmic and the divine converged, shaping an era that resonated with the Piscean energies of love, compassion, and transcendence. The Age of Pisces, marked by Christ's message and mission, became a testament to the cosmic dance between the heavens and human history — a dance that continues to unfold, inviting us to embrace the higher spiritual truths that lie within the embrace of the Fish.

Astrology's Enduring Resilience

Through the fall of empires and the rise of new eras, astrology's enduring resilience was a testament to its profound impact on human understanding. From the ancient Greeks and Romans to the Medieval Arab scholars and Renaissance thinkers, each era brought its own interpretations, refinements, and controversies. Astrology continued to evolve, adapting to the shifting sands of intellectual, cultural, and societal changes

The evolution of astrology did not escape the scrutiny of the modern scientific revolution. As empirical methods gained prominence, astrology faced skepticism and skepticism. However, even as science questioned its validity, astrology persisted, finding a new audience seeking meaning and connection in a rapidly changing world.

CHAPTER 5
ASTROLOGY 101

Revealing the celestial lexicon within the

VAST EXPANSE OF THE COSMOS, astrology emerges as a profound bridge that connects the ethereal realms of the celestial with the tangible landscapes of the terrestrial.

This chapter serves as a compass, pointing toward the foundational principles that illuminate the pathways of this ancient and revered art. Here, we venture into the heart of astrology, peeling back the layers of its essence to reveal the profound language that transcends time and space.

The Zodiac: A Celestial Circle of Influence

The zodiac, a celestial circle that graces the heavens, is a gallery of archetypal portraits, each bearing the signature of a distinct personality—a zodiac sign. Aries, Taurus, Gemini, and beyond— these signs are like cosmic brushstrokes, each revealing its unique hues upon the canvas of human nature. With elemental forces as their foundation, and ruling planets guiding their energies, the zodiac signs form a celestial council that shapes our characters and destiny. As we traverse the zodiac's landscape, we'll unveil the traits, strengths, and tendencies inherent in each sign, as well as the cosmic dance that influences their interconnectedness.

In the boundless expanse above, the planets journey across the sky, each radiating its own distinctive energy—a symphony of cosmic forces. From the fiery passions of Mars to the ethereal intuition of Neptune, each planet embodies a facet of human experience. These celestial messengers herald messages that resonate deeply within us, shaping our behavior, emotions, and aspirations. Through a lens that blends mythology, astronomy, and symbolism, we'll embark on an odyssey among the planets, unraveling their archetypal power and their intimate influence on our lives.

As the planets traverse their orbital pathways, they engage in celestial dialogues, forming intricate geometric relationships known as aspects. These conversations create a celestial symphony, revealing the harmonies and dissonances within the cosmos. From the harmonious trine's fluid melodies to the tension of the square's challenges, we'll explore the nuances of these planetary connections. Just as musical notes create a composition, these aspects weave the intricate tapestry of our lives, shaping the ebb and flow of our experiences.

he cosmic stage upon which the planets perform is divided into twelve houses, each a distinct arena where life's myriad dramas unfold. These houses are the setting for our interactions, experiences, and personal growth. From the foundational first house that represents self-awareness to the mystical twelfth house that symbolizes transcendence, each sector carries its unique energy. Through the windows of the houses, we glimpse the panoramic vista of human existence—a landscape that encompasses everything from career endeavors to relationships, unveiling the cosmic script that shapes our stories

the 12 Zodiacal Signs

Imagine the celestial sphere as a meticulously designed clockwork mechanism, with the twelve astrological signs ingeniously positioned like the perfectly aligned cogs of a grand cosmic timepiece. Each sign occupies a precisely measured 30-degree arc of celestial longitude, culminating in an exquisite circular arrangement. This celestial choreography is not arbitrary; it's meticulously synchronized with the Sun's apparent trajectory across the sky throughout the year.

The genesis and culmination dates of each astrological sign are provided as approximations, a nod to the nuanced dance of cosmic mechanics. This temporal flexibility arises from the inherent variability in pinpointing the exact moment of the March equinox — an astronomical event that marks the inception of Aries. This equinoctial moment, embodying the balance between day and night, serves as the poignant starting point of the zodiacal journey.

With the equinox's arrival, the curtain rises on the cosmic stage, unveiling Aries as the first luminary to grace the scene. Aries, the pioneer and initiator, sets the tone for the zodiac's symphony, followed in harmonious sequence by the other celestial performers. Each sign, an essential character in the astrological narrative, takes its place, imbuing the passage of time with its unique energy, characteristics, and influences.

As the Earth progresses in its orbital choreography, the solar spotlight shifts, signifying the change from one zodiacal persona to another. The intricacies of this alignment are a testament to the divine harmony woven into the cosmic fabric — an intricate ballet that encapsulates the wisdom of ages, offering insights into human nature, relationships, and life's unfolding chapters.

Just as the heavens continue their eternal dance, so too do the astrological signs evolve in their perennial journey across the celestial tapestry.

The twelve zodiacal signs, each encompassing distinct qualities and attributes, align with specific dates throughout the year:

- Aries (March 21 - April 19): The pioneer, full of energy and initiative.
- Taurus (April 20 - May 20): The grounded stabilizer, appreciating material comfort.
- Gemini (May 21 - June 20): The communicator, curious and adaptable.
- Cancer (June 21 - July 22): The empathetic nurturer, attuned to emotions.
- Leo (July 23 - August 22): The charismatic leader, radiating creativity.
- Virgo (August 23 - September 22): The meticulous analyst, keen on details.
- Libra (September 23 - October 22): The harmonizer, seeking balance and justice.
- Scorpio (October 23 - November 21): The intense investigator, delving deep.
- Sagittarius (November 22 - December 21): The explorer, embracing adventure.
- Capricorn (December 22 - January 19): The ambitious achiever, persistent and disciplined.
- Aquarius (January 20 - February 18): The visionary thinker, promoting change.
- Pisces (February 19 - March 20): The intuitive dreamer, deeply empathetic.

The elements of fire and air stand as philosophical counterparts, positioned 180 degrees apart within the realm of Western astrology. Similarly, earth and water elements forge their own contrasting partnership. This symmetrical balance underscores the harmonious equilibrium present in the cosmos.

Interestingly, not all astrological systems adhere to the four-element framework. The Sepher Yetzirah, for instance, extols a vision of divine emanations that feature only three core elements — a manifestation that radiates from a singular, central source. This divergence in elemental interpretation highlights the diverse philosophical landscapes that astrology has woven across cultures and eras.

Intriguingly, the grand tapestry of seasons contributes to this symphony of oppositions. Signs born during the vernal equinox, the hopeful harbingers of spring, stand in stark contrast to their autumn-born counterparts. Similarly, the winter-born signs, cloaked in introspection, mirror the summertime luminaries. This perpetual dance of cosmic duality infuses the zodiacal journey with depth and resonance.

And so, the zodiacal wheel turns, unveiling a profound dance of contrasts. Aries, the fiery initiator, finds itself juxtaposed against Libra, the harmonizing diplomat. Taurus, the steadfast earth sign, stands across from Scorpio, the enigmatic water force. Gemini, the communicative twin, mirrors Sagittarius, the intrepid explorer. Cancer, the nurturing nurturer, is in opposition to Capricorn, the tenacious climber. Leo, the regal sunbearer, casts its opposite gaze toward Aquarius, the innovative visionary. Virgo, the analytical mind, meets its counterpoint in Pisces, the empathetic dreamer. This symphony of oppositions paints the celestial canvas with hues of balance, creating a dance that mirrors the dualities intrinsic to human existence.

The polarity

In the realm of Western astrology, the concept of polarity unfolds as a fundamental division that cleaves the zodiac in half, bestowing it with a nuanced spectrum of energies. This division hinges on the alignment of a sign's fundamental energy, categorizing it as either positive or negative. Within this intricate dynamic, an array of attributes and characteristics naturally flow, delineating each sign's essence.

Positive polarity signs, often synonymous with being active, yang, expressive, or masculine, find their embodiment within the six odd-numbered signs of the zodiac: Aries, Gemini, Leo, Libra, Sagittarius, and Aquarius. These luminaries radiate with a vibrant life force, akin to the fiery fervor of Aries, the communicative curiosity of Gemini, the regal charisma of Leo, the harmonizing diplomacy of Libra, the exploratory enthusiasm of Sagittarius, and the visionary innovation of Aquarius. Collectively, these positive polarity signs coalesce to form the fire and air triplicities, igniting the flames of passion and intellectual engagement.

In harmonious contrast, negative polarity signs, often described as passive, yin, receptive, or feminine, encompass the six even-numbered signs of the zodiac: Taurus, Cancer, Virgo, Scorpio, Capricorn, and Pisces. These signs resonate with the calm embrace of Taurus, the nurturing sensitivity of Cancer, the analytical precision of Virgo, the profound depth of Scorpio, the disciplined determination of Capricorn, and the empathetic intuition of Pisces. Together, they comprise the earth and water triplicities, grounding the zodiac in stability and emotional resonance.

This intricate interplay of polarities weaves a cosmic dance that underlines the intricate duality within creation. As the positive and negative forces intertwine, they form a harmonious equilibrium, reminiscent of the yin-yang symbol's profound wisdom. In the rich tapestry of the zodiac, the polarity concept adds another layer of understanding, infusing each sign with its distinctive energetic resonance, guiding individuals on their personal journeys through the celestial map.

The Three Modalities
Seasons and Cosmic Expression

Within the intricate framework of astrology, the concept of modality unfurls like a key to understanding a sign's disposition and relationship to the seasons. Each of the four elements — fire, earth, air, and water — displays itself through three distinct modalities: cardinal, fixed, and mutable. This threefold division brings forth an elegant dance of energies, shaping the way a sign interacts with the world.

These modalities are more than just cosmic labels; they represent the sign's positioning within its respective season. Just as each season brings a unique energy, the modality of a sign colors its approach to change and action. With each modality comprising four signs, they are aptly known as Quadruplicities — a testament to the symbiotic relationship between these cosmic principles.

To illustrate, consider Aries — the pioneer of the zodiac. It finds its place at the onset of spring in the Northern Hemisphere, a time of rebirth and initiation. As a result, Aries is attributed with a cardinal modality, symbolizing its proclivity for beginnings, leadership, and dynamic action. In contrast, a sign like Capricorn, aligned with the winter solstice, resonates with a cardinal earth modality. This pairing embodies Capricorn's pragmatic and disciplined approach to manifesting its goals in the material world.

This amalgamation of element and modality confers distinct character traits upon each zodiacal sign. The connection between the two is akin to a cosmic fingerprint, lending each sign its unique blend of energies and attributes. The three modalities — the initiatory cardinal, the stable fixed, and the adaptable mutable — form a pivotal bridge that interconnects the zodiacal tapestry, allowing us to explore the diverse expressions of each sign as they harmonize with the ever-changing rhythms of the seasons.

Cardinal: Represented by the symbol /•\, the Cardinal modality encapsulates action, dynamism, initiative, and the sheer force of creation. Aries, the fiery trailblazer, carries the torch of beginnings, while Cancer, the intuitive nurturer, leads with emotional depth. Libra, the harmonizer, seeks equilibrium, and Capricorn, the determined climber, employs pragmatic strategies to conquer challenges.

Fixed: Marked by the symbol ⊟, the Fixed modality signifies resistance, unwavering willpower, and an inclination towards inflexibility. Leo, the radiant sun, exhibits strength in adversity, while Scorpio, the enigmatic detective, channels intense determination. Aquarius, the visionary, holds steadfast to innovative ideals, and Taurus, the earthy guardian, stands resolute in its values.

Mutable: Embodied by the symbol ⌢•, the Mutable modality embodies adaptability, flexibility, and resourcefulness. Sagittarius, the philosophical explorer, embraces change with enthusiasm, while Pisces, the dreamy mystic, flows with the tides of transformation. Gemini, the communicative twin, effortlessly shifts between perspectives, and Virgo, the analytical perfectionist, adjusts with meticulous care.

MODALITY	SYMBOL	FIRE SIGNS	WATER SIGNS	AIR SIGNS	EARTH SIGNS
Cardinal		Aries	Cancer	Libra	Capricorn
Fixed		Leo	Scorpio	Aquarius	Taurus
Mutable		Sagittarius	Pisces	Gemini	Virgo

Unveiling Elemental Dynamics

The ancient philosopher Empedocles, in the profound depths of the fifth century BC, made an indelible mark by identifying the foundational elements of fire, earth, air, and water. He painted a vivid portrait of the universe as a symphony composed of two opposing forces—love and strife—molding these elements into intricate amalgamations that give birth to the diverse tapestry of existence. Within this cosmic ballet, each element stands as an equal entity, crowned with its own realm and imbued with its unique essence. Empedocles intriguingly posited that those born with an almost equal balance of these elements tend to possess heightened intelligence and remarkably precise perceptions — a notion that continues to intrigue modern minds.

This elemental classification beckons the term "triplicities," coined for the exquisite correlation between each classical element and a set of three zodiac signs. As such, the fire, earth, air, and water elements harmoniously converge with these astrological constellations, forming a seamless interplay of cosmic energies. Furthermore, the four astrological elements offer an intriguing parallel to the four personality types that Hippocrates had once postulated — air resembling the sanguine, fire mirroring the choleric, earth embodying the melancholic, and water reflecting the phlegmatic. A contemporary lens perceives the elements not merely as isolated symbols but as the very essence that molds human experiences, a concept encapsulated within the comprehensive keywords presented in the table below.

In modern astrology, the role of the elements has swelled in significance. Many astrologers commence their journey into natal chart interpretation by scrutinizing the elemental balance embedded within the planetary placements, particularly the ascendant signs of the Sun and the Moon, as well as the strategic angles within the chart. This elemental analysis serves as a navigational compass, guiding us through the intricate dance of energies that shape our cosmic existence. As we gaze upon this elemental symphony, we perceive a timeless harmony that underscores the intricate connection between the microcosm of the individual and the macrocosm of the universe.

POLARITY	ELEMENT	SYMBOL	KEYWORDS	SIGN TRIPLICITY
Positive	Fire	△	Assertion, drive, willpower	Aries, Leo, Sagittarius
	Air	⟁	Communication, socialization, conceptualization	Gemini, Libra, Aquarius
Negative	Earth	▽	Practicality, caution, material world	Taurus, Virgo, Capricorn
	Water	▽	Emotion, empathy, sensitivity	Cancer, Scorpio, Pisces

Positive Polarity: Fire and Air

The realm of positive polarity is a realm of assertion, propulsion, and vibrant willpower. Here, fire burns brightly, infusing Aries, Leo, and Sagittarius with an ardent spirit, an unquenchable drive, and the courage to pioneer new frontiers. Simultaneously, air elegantly swirls through Gemini, Libra, and Aquarius, nurturing the domains of communication, socialization, and abstract thinking. These signs resonate with the vibrancy of life's effervescent flow and embrace the world with a zealous spirit.

Negative Polarity: Earth and Water

In the realm of negative polarity, the tides of energy manifest as practicality, sensitivity, and grounding. Earth, represented by Taurus, Virgo, and Capricorn, embodies a steadfast connection to the material world, grounding itself in the realms of stability, caution, and tangible manifestation. Water, flowing through

Cancer, Scorpio, and Pisces, envelopes these signs in the realms of emotion, empathy, and profound sensitivity. These signs embody the depths of human experience, flowing through the currents of intuition and empathetic connection.

As the cosmic currents of positive and negative polarities intermingle with the four foundational elements, a grand tapestry of existence unfurls. This delicate equilibrium, where the flames of assertion meet the breezes of communication and the solidity of the earth fuses with the depths of emotion, presents a holistic portrayal of human experience. In this intricate web, each sign finds its home, guided by its elemental compass, amidst the ever-shifting dance of cosmic energies.

Navigating Celestial Dominion
Rulerships and Dignities

In the intricate web of astrology, the interplay between celestial bodies, zodiac signs, and houses unveils a symphony of relationships that steer the course of our destinies. Rulership stands as a beacon of connection, binding planets to their corresponding signs and houses in a dance of cosmic influence. The foundation of these alliances lies in the alignment of the fundamental nature of the planets with the essence of the signs they oversee.

The conventional rulerships forge an eloquent bridge between celestial entities and their earthly reflections. This cosmic harmony emerges in the form of Aries guided by the martial might of Mars, Taurus basking in the tender embrace of Venus, and Gemini being the domain of Mercury's intellectual prowess. The ethereal dance continues with Cancer being cradled in the lunar embrace, Leo radiating with the solar essence, and Virgo under the tutelage of Mercury's analytical finesse. Libra flourishes in the Venusian realm, Scorpio delves into the transformative domain of Pluto, while Sagittarius soars under Jupiter's expansive gaze. Capricorn finds its grounding in the structured dominion of Saturn, Aquarius thrives in the electrifying presence of Uranus, and Pisces is enveloped by the dreamy touch of Neptune.

In astrology's ancient tapestry, dignity and detriment create an exquisite interplay that molds the planets' influence in each sign. The concept of essential dignity posits that planets are most potent in certain signs due to a harmonious resonance between their intrinsic nature and the sign's attributes. A planet gains strength and is dignified when it occupies the sign it rules — like the Moon reigning in Cancer, radiating power. Conversely, a planet's energy is weakened or falls into detriment when it finds itself in the sign opposite its rulership — akin to the Moon's diminished influence in Capricorn. This intricate dance of dignity and detriment paints a portrait of cosmic dynamics that shape astrological interpretations.

Further nuances in the planetary journey are unveiled through exaltation and fall. Exaltation elevates a planet's influence when it occupies a particular sign, conferring a dignified status just below rulership. It's akin to being an honored guest — center-stage, yet confined in potency. Saturn soars in Libra, the Sun finds majesty in Aries, Venus flourishes in Piscean waters, and the Moon radiates in Taurus' embrace. But the flip side emerges with the notion of fall — when a planet is placed in the sign opposing its exaltation. This position signifies a weakened state, amplifying the delicate balance between celestial influence and terrestrial outcomes.

In astrology's symphony, rulership, dignity, and detriment harmonize, evoking the grand orchestration of cosmic energies that compose the narratives of our lives. As planets traverse the heavens, they imprint their essence onto the signs they touch, etching the poetry of destiny onto the canvas of existence.

Sun

With a regal emblem representing its brilliance, the Sun finds its zenith in the sign of Leo, basking in its own majestic rule. Here, the Sun's energy resonates most potently, a beacon of light and vitality. Yet, as the Sun journeys through Aquarius, its influence wanes, encountering a decrease in dignity. The exaltation of the Sun unfurls in Aries, where it radiates fiery vigor, but at the nadir of Libra, the Sun's potency wanes.

Moon

Guiding the tides of emotions, the Moon embraces Cancer with maternal grace, achieving its zenith of influence. However, its journey through Capricorn brings a decrease in dignity, causing a slight diminution of its nurturing energy. The exaltation of the Moon shines in Taurus, where emotions flourish, yet Scorpio marks its fall, subtly veiling its nurturing essence.

Mercury

Mercury, the winged messenger, asserts its dominion over Gemini and Virgo, soaring with increased dignity in its house of thought and communication. Yet, as it journeys through Sagittarius and Pisces, its power diminishes in the realm of philosophy and dreams. Virgo becomes the stage of Mercury's exaltation, where its analytical prowess flourishes, while Pisces serves as its fall, impeding the clarity of thought.

Venus

In the realms of love and beauty, Venus finds its dignified abode in Libra and Taurus, weaving harmonious connections and sensuality. Aries and Scorpio mark the domain of its detriment, where the balance between passion and harmony is unsettled. Pisces exalts Venus in a romantic embrace, while Virgo's precision becomes its fall.

Mars

Mars, the warrior planet, asserts itself in Aries and Scorpio, wielding heightened influence as it navigates themes of action and transformation. Libra and Taurus represent its houses of decrease, where conflict and energy find a less harmonious expression. The exaltation of Mars unfurls in Capricorn, where disciplined ambition reigns supreme, while Cancer marks its fall, veiling its assertive energy.

Jupiter

Jupiter's expansive energy thrives in Sagittarius and Pisces, as it embarks on a journey of philosophical growth and spiritual enlightenment. As it dances through Gemini and Virgo, its influence contracts, diminishing its potential for expansion. The exaltation of Jupiter radiates in Cancer, nurturing benevolent growth, while Capricorn symbolizes its fall, restraining its expansive tendencies.

Saturn

Saturn, the stern teacher of the cosmos, finds its dignified dominion in Capricorn and Aquarius, embodying discipline and structure. As it traverses Cancer and Leo, its influence weakens, questioning its role in nurturing and self-expression. Libra becomes Saturn's exalted throne of wisdom, but its power wanes in the fall of Aries.

Planet Books and Cosmic Influences

Within the pages of "planet books," a genre that emerged in the mid-15th century in the Alemannic German region, the cosmic interplay of the Ptolemaic planets and human existence is meticulously charted. These treatises, adorned with intricate illustrations, offer a glimpse into the influence of each planet upon those born "under their reign." As these manuscripts proliferated, they became an emblem of the German Renaissance's fascination with celestial iconography, extending their impact well into the 17th century.

In the intricate world of astrology, where celestial bodies weave a cosmic dance, the concept of accidental dignity emerges as a crucial facet in the tapestry of interpretation. Unlike essential dignity, which derives from a planet's zodiacal position, accidental dignity is the planet's "ability to act," influenced by its house placement within the examined chart. This intricate interplay of essential and accidental dignity brings depth and complexity to astrological analysis.

For instance, envision the Moon in Cancer, dignified by its rulership, yet confined to the 12th house — an abode that mutes its expression. Cadent houses, including the 3rd, 6th, and 9th, along with the 12th, are considered weak or afflicted, hindering the planet's efficacy. Contrarily, the Moon in the 1st, 4th, 7th, or 10th house exudes greater influence, residing in angular houses that amplify its capacity to act. Planets positioned in succedent houses like the 2nd, 5th, 8th, and 11th exhibit moderate potency. Accidental dignity delves into how a planet manifests its energy based on its chart placement, offering a dynamic layer of insight.

The distinction between accidental and essential dignity mirrors the contrast between a planet's inherent nature and its capacity to express that nature. Consider a valuable ring as a significator in a horary question. While it possesses good essential dignity due to its value, its accidental dignity might be diminished if it's lost—a poignant example of how circumstances can influence a planet's power to act.

Accidental dignity can be bestowed upon a planet through various avenues. Most notably, a planet gains accidental dignity when positioned on an angle—Ascendant, Midheaven, Descendant, or IC. Additionally, direct motion and swiftness enhance a planet's accidental dignity, as does liberation from combustion or being in cazimi—a celestial embrace with the Sun. When a planet forms a harmonious aspect with a fortunate planet or aligns with a benevolent fixed star, its accidental dignity is augmented.

In horary and electional astrology, essential and accidental dignity serve as guiding stars. They illuminate the potency of planets, navigating practitioners through the labyrinthine intricacies of interpretation. The blend of these dignities unveils the nuanced interplay between cosmic energies and human destinies, turning the astrological chart into a profound map of possibilities.

Mastery classification

In the intricate tapestry of astrology, additional classifications deepen our understanding of the zodiac's profound intricacies. One such classification is the division of each zodiac sign into three distinct 10° segments known as decans or decanates. While these divisions may have waned in contemporary astrological discourse, their historical significance remains invaluable. The first decanate, harmoniously resonating with the core nature of its parent sign, is believed to encapsulate that sign's essence most emphatically. Governed by the sign ruler, it holds a unique and potent energy.

The subsequent decanate steps into the realm of the adjacent sign, carrying the sub-rulership of the planet governing the next sign within the same triplicity. This transitional influence subtly alters the expression of the sign's characteristics, allowing a spectrum of nuances to emerge. Completing this trio, the last decanate is under the influence of the next sign in sequence within the same triplicity. This sequential arrangement weaves a narrative of continuous evolution, where the energies transition and transform seamlessly from one decanate to the next.

Delving deeper into the symphony of the zodiac, the combination of element and modality provides another layer of classification. While the element and modality of a sign inherently define its essential nature, these traits can be grouped to convey broader symbolism. The initial quartet of signs — Aries, Taurus, Gemini, and Cancer — constitutes the domain of personal signs. Here, the emphasis is on self-discovery, personal identity, and the individual's journey of growth.

Transitioning into the next set — Leo, Virgo, Libra, and Scorpio — we encounter the sphere of interpersonal signs. These signs delve into matters of relationships, communication, and the intricate dance between self and others. This quadrant delves into the dynamics of partnerships, interactions, and the subtleties of human connection.

Finally, the last segment — Sagittarius, Capricorn, Aquarius, and Pisces — encompasses the realm of transpersonal signs. These signs reach beyond the individual and tap into the collective consciousness, embracing universal ideals and concepts. Themes of spirituality, empathy, and altruism are highlighted, as these signs explore the interconnectedness of all beings and the cosmic fabric that unites us.

SİGN	SYMBOL	SUN START DATES	SUN SİGN END DATES	İPTİC LONGİT (a ≤ λ < b)	HOUSE	POLARİTY
ARİES	♈□	21 March	20-apr	0° to 30°	1	Positive
TAURUS	♉□	21 April	21 May	30° to 60°	2	Negative
GEMİNİ	♊□	22 May	21 June	60° to 90°	3	Positive
CANCER	♋□	22 June	23 July	90° to 120°	4	Negative
LEO	♌□	24 July	23 August	120° to 150°	5	Positive
VİRGO	♍□	24 August	23 September	150° to 180°	6	Negative
LİBRA	♎□	24 September	23 October	180° to 210°	7	Positive
SCORPİO	♏□	24 October	22 November	210° to 240°	8	Negative
SAGİTTARİUS	♐□	23 November	21 December	240° to 270°	9	Positive
CAPRİCORN	♑□	22 December	20 January	270° to 300°	10	Negative
AQUARİUS	♒□	21 January	19 February	300° to 330°	11	Positive
PİSCES	♓□	20 February	20 March	330° to 360°	12	Negative

SİGN	SYMBOL	MODALİTY	TRİPLİCİTY	NORTH	SOUTHERN	MODERN RULER	CLASSİC
ARİES	♈□	Cardinal	Fire	Spring	Autumn	Mars	
TAURUS	♉□	Fixed	Earth	Spring	Autumn	Venus	
GEMİNİ	♊□	Mutable	Air	Spring	Autumn	Mercury	
CANCER	♋□	Cardinal	Water	Summer	Winter	Moon	
LEO	♌□	Fixed	Fire	Summer	Winter	Sun	
VİRGO	♍□	Mutable	Earth	Summer	Winter	Mercury	
LİBRA	♎□	Cardinal	Air	Autumn	Spring	Venus	
SCORPİO	♏□	Fixed	Water	Autumn	Spring	Pluto (or)	Mars
SAGİTTARİUS	♐□	Mutable	Fire	Autumn	Spring	Jupiter	
CAPRİCORN	♑□	Cardinal	Earth	Winter	Summer	Saturn	
AQUARİUS	♒□	Fixed	Air	Winter	Summer	Uranus	Saturn
PİSCES	♓□	Mutable	Water	Winter	Summer	Neptune	Jupiter

Understanding the Planetary Forces
Celestial Messengers of Influence

In the vast tapestry of the cosmos, the celestial messengers known as planets take center stage, embodying profound cosmic forces that intricately interlace with every facet of our lives. These wanderers, each a unique entity in the cosmic ballet, serve as conduits for universal energies that shape our human experience. In their ceaseless orbits, they communicate messages of significance and deliver distinct energies that resonate with various aspects of our existence.

Imagine the planets as emissaries, each donning a cloak of symbolism and meaning. Like characters in a grand play, they carry narratives of purpose and influence that guide us through the intricate dance of life. Each planet wields its own set of keys, playing chords that resonate within our souls and stir our motivations, aspirations, and actions. Just as a skilled musician can evoke emotions through the piano's notes, the planets strike chords within us, setting the stage for our experiences.

Through the lens of astrology, we decode these planetary archetypes to uncover the inner workings of our motivations, desires, and the unfolding events that shape our reality. By understanding the unique energies associated with each celestial envoy, we gain a profound insight into the intricate tapestry of our own nature. The dance of the planets influences the cosmic symphony of our lives, prompting us to explore our potentials, face challenges, and navigate the currents of existence with greater awareness.

In this exploration of the planets' influences, we gain not only self-awareness but also a deeper connection to the grandeur of the universe. Each planet paints its stroke upon the canvas of our lives, contributing to the masterpiece that is our journey. As we embrace their teachings and align ourselves with their energies, we harmonize with the rhythm of the cosmos, allowing the celestial messengers to guide us on a voyage of self-discovery, growth, and transformation.

The planetary pantheon

In the cosmos' celestial ballet, the planets hold their roles as cosmic deities, each intricately woven into the fabric of human existence. These planetary beings, carrying the names of ancient gods and embodying their unique attributes, impart profound insights into the realms of human emotion, behavior, and destiny. As we embark on a journey through the planetary pantheon, we unveil the rich tapestry of connections that shape our lives, both on earthly and celestial planes.

Sun: The Radiant Sol

Radiating its brilliance across cultures and epochs, the Sun is Sol, Helios, Shamash, and Surya—the bringer of light and life. As Apollo's chariot races across the heavens, Ra's powerful rays pierce the darkness, illuminating the path of divination and prophecy. The Sun is not just a celestial body but the embodiment of ego, purpose, and vitality—a beacon of inspiration that guides us toward our inner truth and identity.

Moon: The Enigmatic Luna

Selene, Sin, Chandra—the Moon enchants with its silvery glow, evoking Artemis' huntress spirit and Khonsu's celestial wisdom. As Diana roams the night, the Moon reflects our emotional tides, nurturing our deepest connections and maternal instincts. Luna's phases mirror the ebb and flow of our lives, casting its ethereal glow upon our dreams and innermost feelings.

Mercury: The Swift Messenger

Known by many names—Hermes, Nabu, Budha, Thoth—
Mercury weaves communication's tapestry across cultures. The
messenger of the gods, Mercury guides us through the realms of
intellect, wit, and cleverness. As the divine patron of travel and
commerce, Mercury bestows its blessing upon our exchanges,
ensuring that ideas and thoughts flow freely like the swift
currents of its cosmic dance.

Venus: The Goddess of Love

Aphrodite, Inanna, Shukra—Venus reigns over the domains of
love, romance, and aesthetics. The goddess of beauty, fertility,
and desire, Venus empowers our connections and artistic
endeavors. As Hathor's nurturing touch and Isis' allure
intertwine, Venus ignites the flames of passion, evoking
emotions that transform the heart's canvas into a masterpiece of
love.

Mars: The Warrior Spirit

Ares, Nergal, Mangala—the fiery essence of Mars embodies the
warrior archetype, summoning the spirit of battle and conquest.
Born of Earth's strength, Mars incites our drive, aggression, and
determination. This celestial general, a son of the soil, enkindles
our passions, fortitude, and the assertive energy that fuels our
endeavors.

Jupiter: The Benevolent King

Jove, Dias, Marduk, Guru—the jovial majesty of Jupiter reigns as
a kingly presence. A ruler and father among gods, Jupiter
exudes wisdom, expansion, and fortune. Brihaspati's divine
teachings echo in Jupiter's guidance, nurturing our luck and

spirituality. As this cosmic mentor shapes our growth, Jupiter's jovial dance ignites the sparks of optimism and expansion.

Saturn: The Timeless Reaper

Cronus, Kajamanu, Shani—Saturn, the god of agriculture, manifests as the cosmic keeper of time and karma. With the wisdom of age, Saturn administers discipline, structure, and life's inevitable consequences. Shani Dev's just hand guides us through hardships, fostering ambition and patience, while shaping our destinies with lessons of resilience and honor.

Uranus: The Cosmic Innovator

Ouranos, Anshar, Aruna—Uranus stands as the innovator of the zodiac, igniting eccentricity, originality, and change. Charioteer of the Sun, Uranus challenges conventions, electrifying our lives with unexpected transformations. In its celestial dance, Uranus bestows the gifts of revolution and liberation, sparking the fires of change that illuminate our journey.

Neptune: The Mystic Voyager

Poseidon, Enki, Varuna—Neptune, the god of the sea, draws us into the realm of dreams, illusions, and the unseen. As Khnum molds the clay of our subconscious, Neptune invites us to explore the depths of our psyche. Through its watery currents, Neptune bridges the realms of reality and fantasy, inspiring psychic receptivity and artistic expression.

Pluto: The Regenerator of Souls

Plouton, Ereshkigal, Yama—Pluto, the lord of the underworld, embodies the cycles of death and rebirth. A guardian of the abyss, Pluto draws us into the mysteries of transformation, wielding its power to uncover hidden truths. With Osiris' guidance, Pluto delves into our subconscious forces, inviting us to shed the old and embrace the new, fostering our spiritual evolution.

Planetary Legacies and Human Traits

The Ptolemaic planets bequeath their distinctive traits to their earthly children, crafting a mosaic of human attributes that mirror their celestial patrons. Saturn's legacy bestows industriousness, melancholy, and tranquility. Jupiter's grace infuses charm and a penchant for the hunt. Mars' influence breeds the spirit of the soldier and the warrior's art. The Sun's radiant rays gift the realms of music and athleticism. The tender Moon bequeaths shyness and a tender heart. Mercury's realm embodies prudence, cleverness, love, and commerce. Lastly, Venus' ethereal touch awakens amorousness and passionate fervor.

Alchemy: Bridging the Celestial and the Earthly

In the sacred space of alchemy, the planets' influence is not merely a historical relic but a bridge connecting the cosmic and the human. As alchemists strive to transmute the base into the sublime, these planetary influences guide their spiritual journey, leading them to uncover the hidden truths of the universe and the self. The planets become a language through which alchemists converse with the cosmos, seeking wisdom, transformation, and unity in their eternal dance.

Unveiling the Cosmic Conversation
the planetary aspects

planets engage in a celestial dialogue through a language of angles known as aspects. These angles, formed by the positions of planets in relation to each other and key points in the horoscope, offer insights into the intricate dance of energies that shape our lives.

These angles are measured in degrees and minutes of ecliptic longitude, revealing the conversations between celestial beings. The Ascendant, Midheaven, Descendant, and other points of astrological interest join this cosmic discourse, marking moments of transition and developmental change in the human experience.

astrological aspects were often categorized as either beneficial (benefic) or detrimental (malefic). However, modern astrology places less emphasis on such distinctions, embracing a more nuanced approach. This is exemplified by the exploration of astrological harmonics, an idea championed by Johannes Kepler in his 1619 book "Harmonice Mundi." John Addey continued this exploration, contributing to the understanding of aspects' subtle interplay.

Deep within the annals of astrology lies the legacy of Ptolemy, an ancient sage whose insights into the cosmos continue to shape our understanding of the celestial dance. The Ptolemaic Aspects, introduced by Ptolemy in the 1st Century AD, stand as pillars of astrological wisdom, unveiling a tapestry of angles that weave the very fabric of our destinies.

Ptolemy's genius lies in his ability to distill the intricate relationships between celestial bodies into a set of major aspects, often referred to as Ptolemaic Aspects. These angles, carefully defined and refined by his wisdom, offer a profound glimpse into the language of the cosmos. These aspects are Conjunction (0°), Sextile (60°), Square (90°), Trine (120°), and Opposition (180°). Anchored in mathematical precision, these aspects embody the ancient art of celestial interpretation.

The beauty of Ptolemaic Aspects lies in their harmony with the cosmic circle. Divisible by 10 and evenly distributed within the 360° celestial sphere, these aspects hold a balance and symmetry that resonates with the cosmic order. The Conjunction aligns forces as one, the Sextile and Trine bring ease and opportunity, the Square challenges for growth, and the Opposition creates tension for reflection.

Yet, in the labyrinthine world of astrology, no stone goes unturned. The concept of orbs adds an intricate layer of interpretation to these aspects. Orbs define the acceptable degree of separation between exactitude for an aspect to hold its influence. The wisdom of orbs adapts to the astrologer's needs and the intricacies of the chart, reflecting the artistry of interpretation.

Let's delve deeper into the fascinating world of some of the most fundamental aspects: Conjunction, Opposition, Sextile, Square, and Trine.

Conjunction: The Cosmic Embrace

A Conjunction, marked by an angle of approximately 0–10°, is a celestial embrace where planets stand side by side, merging their energies into a singular force. This aspect wields immense power, acting as a cosmic amplifier that intensifies the effects of the involved planets. It's as if the planets whisper their secrets to one another, fostering a profound connection. Beneficial Conjunctions involving luminaries like the Sun, Venus, and Jupiter may bestow gifts of charm and opportunity, while challenging ones involving the Moon, Mars, or Saturn might present hurdles to overcome.

The Stellium

celestial bodies align to create unique configurations that hold profound astrological significance. One such configuration is the stellium—a convergence of three or more planets within a narrow segment of the zodiac. This cosmic phenomenon weaves together the energies of these planets, infusing a particular area of a birth chart with intensified influence and complex dynamics.

This clustering creates a concentration of energies, resulting in a powerful focal point within an individual's birth chart. Stelliums are known for magnifying the traits associated with the involved signs and planets, amplifying their effects in the person's life.

Opposition: Dance of Dichotomy

An Opposition, spanning 180°, is a cosmic dance of opposites, mirroring the dualities of life. This aspect embodies tension and polarization, compelling us to navigate through contrasting forces. Unlike the unifying nature of a Conjunction, an Opposition holds a relational quality, symbolizing externalization and potential exaggeration. It's a cosmic tango where planets engage in a dramatic dialogue, and its energies are integral to interpreting relationships and conflicts in a chart.

Sextile: The Harmonious Conversation

A Sextile, formed by a 60° angle, is a harmonious conversation between planets that fosters compatibility and ease. It's like two friends sitting down for a heart-to-heart chat, promoting understanding and cooperation. Although less intense than a Trine, a Sextile offers a golden opportunity for growth and communication. By exerting a little effort, individuals can tap into this aspect's potential, enhancing connections between different elements of their lives.

Square: Forging Pathways of Growth

A Square, at 90°, is a cosmic crucible of tension that forges pathways of growth. It's akin to a crossroads where important decisions must be made, often involving trade-offs between opportunities and challenges. This aspect can propel individuals to action, encouraging them to navigate through obstacles and make pivotal choices. While it can create inner conflict, the Square is a catalyst for change, urging us to overcome difficulties and evolve.

Trine: Harmonic Flow

A Trine, encompassing 120°, blesses charts with a harmonious flow of energy. It's a celestial connection that signifies ease, talent, and natural alignment. Like a gentle stream meandering through the landscape, a Trine bestows innate gifts and opportunities. It's an aspect of grace, suggesting that events unfold effortlessly, often emerging from current or past situations in a smooth and natural manner.

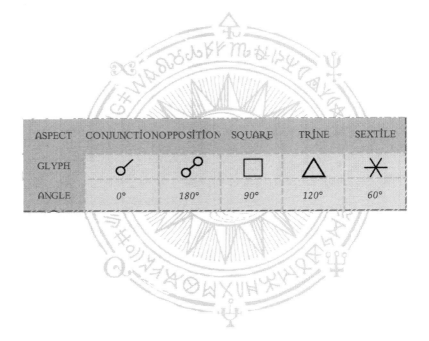

ASPECT	CONJUNCTION	OPPOSITION	SQUARE	TRINE	SEXTILE
GLYPH	☌	☍	□	△	✶
ANGLE	0°	180°	90°	120°	60°

Great conjuctions

Throughout history, the grand dance between the slowest-moving classical planets, Jupiter and Saturn, has captivated the human imagination as a celestial harbinger of change. The fascination with these Great Conjunctions has deep roots, tracing back to Arabic translations and ancient manuscripts that made their way to Europe, notably Albumasar's work on Conjunctions. From the late Middle Ages to the Renaissance, the allure of these celestial omens found a place in the musings of scholars, philosophers, and even literary luminaries like Dante and Shakespeare.

The Great Conjunctions occur approximately every 20 years, charting a mesmerizing retrograde path of about 120° across the sky. When observed over time, these Conjunctions form triangular patterns that repeat after every third occurrence. It's as if the planets are painting cosmic triangles in the heavens, a visual spectacle that returns to the vicinity of its origin after around 60 years. This cyclical phenomenon, however, doesn't quite align with the fixed stars due to a shift of about 8°. Moreover, only a maximum of four Conjunctions may happen in the same zodiac sign.

Astrologers have bestowed significant importance on the placement of Great Conjunctions within the three Triplicities or Trigons of Zodiac signs. These triangular patterns are associated with one of four elements, and the initiation of a new Trigon holds particular significance, occurring approximately every 240 years. When all four Trigons have been visited, a new cycle commences, marking a cosmic event that takes place around 900 years.

In 1606, Johannes Kepler's book, entitled as De Stella Nova, illustrated the Trigons of Great Conjunctions.

Medieval astrologers, using the Alphonsine tables, calculated a cycle of 960 years, factoring in the time it took for the Conjunctions to move from one trigon to the next. However, if measured by the Conjunctions' return to the same right ascension rather than the same constellation, the cycle is shorter, around 800 years due to axial precession. The exact duration has been a subject of debate, with Kepler estimating it at 794 years, leading to 40 Conjunctions.

Until the late 16th century, the anticipation and belief in the transformative power of these events fueled a steady stream of publications. The year 1583 marked the final Conjunction in the watery trigon, sparking widespread speculation about apocalyptic changes. In response, a Papal Bull was issued in 1586 against such divinations.

ELEMENT	CONJUNCTION 1			CONJUNCTION 2			CONJUNCTION 3		
	SIGN	SYMBOL	ECLIPTIC LONGITUDE	SIGN	SYMBOL	ECLIPTIC LONGITUDE	SIGN	SYMBOL	ECLIPTIC LONGITUDE
FIRE TRIGON	Aries	♈	1 (0° to 30°)	Leo	♌	5 (120° to 150°)	Sagittarius	♐	9 (240° to 270°)
EARTH TRIGON	Taurus	♉	2 (30° to 60°)	Virgo	♍	6 (150° to 180°)	Capricorn	♑	10 (270° to 300°)
AIR TRIGON	Gemini	♊	3 (60° to 90°)	Libra	♎	7 (180° to 210°)	Aquarius	♒	11 (300° to 330°)
WATER TRIGON	Cancer	♋	4 (90° to 120°)	Scorpio	♏	8 (210° to 240°)	Pisces	♓	12 (330° to 360°)

Fire Trigon:

The fiery arc commences with Aries, its symbol representing the brave ram, boldly charging through the ecliptic at 0° to 30°. This initiatory force is then carried forth by the radiant lion, Leo, taking its stance between 120° and 150°. Finally, Sagittarius adds its dynamic energy to the fire trigon, blazing in the cosmos from 240° to 270°. Together, these fire signs ignite the spirit, fueling passion, inspiration, and unquenchable enthusiasm.

Earth Trigon:

Grounded in stability and practicality, the earth trigon commences with Taurus, symbolized by the steadfast bull, serenely grazing through the ecliptic from 30° to 60°. Virgo follows suit, gracefully tending to the earth's bounties at 150° to 180°. Completing this elemental trio is Capricorn, ascending to the zenith of the sky from 270° to 300°. Through these earth signs, the essence of manifestation, growth, and groundedness finds its expression.

Air Trigon:

The airy cadence begins with Gemini, represented by the twin figures in eternal conversation, bridging the space between 60° and 90°. Libra follows, the elegant scales of balance swaying harmoniously from 180° to 210°. Completing this ethereal trio is Aquarius, the water bearer, pouring wisdom and innovation into the celestial sphere from 300° to 330°. The air signs infuse the atmosphere with intellect, communication, and the spirit of cooperation.

Water Trigon:

Flowing with emotional depth and intuition, the water trigon emerges with Cancer, the tender crab, navigating the emotional currents from 90° to 120°. Scorpio follows, the enigmatic scorpion, delving into the mysteries of life between 210° and 240°. Finally, Pisces, the two fish swimming in opposite directions, merges the realms of reality and imagination from 330° to 360°. These water signs invite us to explore the realm of feelings, intuition, and the subconscious.

CHAPTER 6
THE COSMIC ENGINE -
SET STARS IN MOTION

OUR BIRTH CHART IS THE INTRICATE

CHOREOGRAPHY OF YOUR LIFE. It's a snapshot of the celestial positions at the exact moment of your birth, a unique blueprint that sets the stars in motion within you. As we delve into this chapter, you'll come to understand the birth chart as the cosmic engine that drives your journey on this earthly stage.

Picture the universe as a grand stage, and your birth chart as the script that defines your role in the cosmic play. Just as no two actors bring the same interpretation to a character, your birth chart reveals your individuality and purpose in this world. It's a map of your potential, a guide to your strengths, and a reflection of your challenges.

Your birth chart consists of twelve houses, each representing a different area of your life, and ten planets, including the Sun and the Moon, each embodying unique energies. These planets reside within the twelve zodiac signs, each carrying its own qualities and characteristics. Together, these elements weave the rich tapestry of your personality and destiny.

The birth chart

The art of calculating birth charts has come a long way from its humble beginnings. In ancient times, astrologers meticulously crafted these intricate celestial maps by hand, using little more than a protractor and an ephemeris, a table of planetary positions over time. This painstaking process required immense skill and precision.

Before the digital age, the ephemeris was the astrologer's trusty companion, akin to a cosmic almanac. It contained a treasure trove of data, listing the positions of celestial bodies for each day of the year. With this invaluable resource, astrologers could calculate birth charts and make astrological predictions. It was a labor-intensive task, involving meticulous calculations that required an astute understanding of celestial mechanics.

One of the most remarkable aspects of birth chart calculations is their sensitivity to time. The birth chart is like a cosmic fingerprint, unique to each individual, and it shifts with incredible speed. Every four minutes, the celestial bodies move to form new angles and aspects. This rapid movement underscores the importance of an accurate time of birth.

In the modern era, the digital revolution transformed the field of astrology. With the advent of astrology software, the complex calculations once performed by hand became nearly instantaneous. Astrologers and enthusiasts could now access a vast database of celestial data with ease. This technology not only made the process more efficient but also reduced the margin of error.

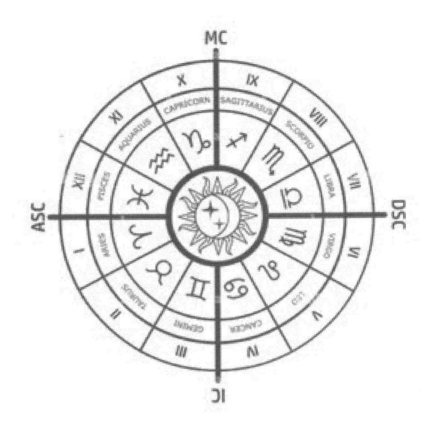

The chart is divided into twelve segments, called houses, each representing specific life areas or themes. To understand the horizon line (also known as the Ascendant-Descendant axis) and the zenith line (or Midheaven-Imum Coeli axis) of the birth chart wheel, we'll explore these two significant axes:

Horizon Line (Ascendant-Descendant Axis):

The horizon line is an essential element in the birth chart. It represents the line where the sky appears to meet the Earth's surface at the time of your birth.

- The Ascendant (AC), or Rising Sign, marks the eastern point of the horizon. It's the sign that was rising on the eastern horizon at the moment you were born.
- The Descendant (DC) is the opposite point on the western horizon, signifying the sign that was setting at your birth.
- The Ascendant, often considered the most important point in the chart, represents how you present yourself to the world, your outward behavior, and your approach to life.
- The Descendant is associated with your interactions with others, particularly in close relationships. It often reflects the qualities you seek in a partner or how you relate to others on a one-on-one basis.

Zenith Line (Midheaven-Imum Coeli Axis):

The zenith line, also known as the Midheaven-Imum Coeli (MC-IC) axis, runs perpendicular to the horizon line.

- The Midheaven (MC) is located at the top of the chart (twelve o'clock position), marking the highest point in the sky at the time of your birth.

- The Imum Coeli (IC) is situated at the bottom of the chart (six o'clock position), representing the lowest point in the sky.
- The Midheaven is associated with your career, public image, aspirations, and how you present yourself in the professional world.
- The Imum Coeli reflects your roots, family life, home environment, and your inner foundation. It signifies your private, personal life.

Understanding the horizon line and zenith line in your birth chart provides valuable insights into the balance between your public and private life, your relationships, and your career aspirations. These axes, along with the placement of planets, zodiac signs, and houses, create a rich tapestry of information that astrologers use to provide insights into your personality, life path, and potential challenges and opportunities.

The Sun's position in the chart reflects whether it was daytime or nighttime when you were born.

When the Sun is above the horizon line (Ascendant-Descendant axis), it symbolizes that you were born during the daytime. This means the Sun was visible in the sky when you took your first breath.

Conversely, when the Sun is below the horizon line, it represents nighttime. This indicates that you were born when the Sun had set, and it was dark outside.

Zenith (Midday) and Nadir (Midnight):

In addition to day and night, the Sun's position in relation to the meridian line (Midheaven-Imum Coeli axis) provides insights into specific times of the day.

When the Sun is located at the top of the birth chart, on or near the meridian line (Midheaven), it signifies that the Sun is at its zenith. This corresponds to midday, when the Sun is at its highest point in the sky, and it is directly overhead.

On the other hand, when the Sun is positioned at the bottom of the birth chart, close to the meridian line (Imum Coeli), it represents the Sun at its nadir. This corresponds to midnight, when the Sun is at its lowest point below the horizon.

Understanding the Sun's position in your birth chart regarding the horizon line and the meridian line helps astrologers interpret the time of day or night and whether the Sun was at its zenith (midday) or nadir (midnight) when you were born. These factors add depth to the astrological analysis and provide valuable information about your life path, tendencies, and potential life events.

(also asc, represent the east point and desc the west point of cardinal points, zenith is south and nadir nord)

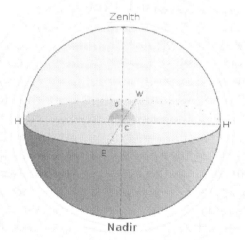

The 12 houses

Imagine the birth chart as a captivating mosaic, comprised of 12 unique sections, each with its own profound story to tell. These segments, known as "houses," are not to be confused with the zodiac signs, although both share the number 12 in common. The houses offer a distinct perspective, a deep dive into the intricacies of your life's journey.

As you traverse the birth chart wheel from left to right, you embark on a voyage through the various houses, each unveiling a unique facet of your existence. The journey is akin to moving from the deeply personal and palpable aspects of life to the more abstract and universal realms.

Here's a closer look at the transition from one house to another, revealing the diversity of life experiences they encapsulate:

1st House: Self, Identity, Physical Appearance - At the inception of the chart, the 1st house takes center stage. It reflects your self-image, identity, and how you present yourself to the world, much like the rising sun.

2nd House: Material Possessions, Money, Values - Moving onwards, this house delves into your relationship with material wealth, personal values, and what you truly treasure.

3rd House: Peers, Communication, Siblings - Here, communication, early education, and interactions with siblings become the focal points of your life's narrative.

4th House: Home, Family, Origins - The 4th house uncovers the deepest roots of your existence, including family dynamics, home life, and your sense of belonging.

5th House: Creativity, Romance, Children - As you progress, creativity, romantic endeavors, and the joys of parenthood come into play.

6th House: Health, Wellness, Routines - Health, daily routines, and your work environment become paramount here, grounding you in the realm of practicality.

7th House: Partnership, Contracts, Marriage - This house spotlights relationships, partnerships, and the intricate dance of one-on-one connections.

8th House: Inheritances, Sex, Transformation - Deep transformation, shared resources, and matters of intimacy come to the forefront.

9th House: Philosophy, Travel, Higher Education - Your quest for knowledge, spirituality, and exploration takes flight in the 9th house.

10th House: Career, Legacy, Reputation - As you approach the zenith of the chart, your career, public image, and societal standing come under scrutiny.

11th House: Activism, Technology, Humanitarianism - Friendships, social networks, and your role in larger groups shine brightly here, igniting your passion for change.

12th House: Intuition, Secrets, Spirituality - Finally, you reach the enigmatic 12th house, a realm of intuition, hidden matters, and the profound depths of the subconscious.

Every house serves as a unique backdrop for the stories of your life. Whether or not a planet resides within a house, each plays an integral role in your cosmic narrative. As you explore the intricate web of your birth chart, you'll discover the rich tapestry of your existence, woven together by the interplay of these 12 celestial houses.

Get all together
nterpreting the Birth Chart - Unraveling the Cosmic Tapestry

Now that you've delved into the intricacies of birth chart wheel anatomy and understand the role of houses, planets, and zodiac signs, you're poised to embark on the profound journey of interpreting the celestial map that is your birth chart.

"THE SİMPLE YET MAGİCAL FORMULA:
PLANET + SİGN + HOUSE

Interpreting your birth chart is akin to deciphering a cosmic code that unveils the mysteries of your life's narrative. The formula for this astrological decoding is refreshingly straightforward: Planet + Sign + House. This trio of elements forms the core of astrological analysis, providing insights into what a planet signifies, how it expresses itself through its zodiac sign, and where it manifests its energies within the birth chart's houses.

ASTROLOGY
FOR BEGINNERS

Formula breakdown

Planet: The first component represents the celestial actor, the planet, which carries its unique energy and symbolism. Whether it's the fiery motivation of Mars or the intuitive sensitivity of the Moon, each planet brings its own essence to the cosmic stage.

Sign: The zodiac sign in which the planet resides colors its expression. For instance, Mars in Virgo infuses motivation with meticulousness, while the Moon in Sagittarius imbues emotions with a spirit of exploration.

House: The house placement of the planet provides the stage or arena in which its energies are channeled. For instance, if Mars in Virgo is in the third house, it suggests that your drive and determination are channeled through your interactions, communication, and immediate environment.

Crafting Astrological Narratives

With this formula in your astrological toolkit, you're ready to craft narratives that unveil the unique tapestry of your birth chart. Each combination of planet, sign, and house forms a distinct story thread, weaving together the intricate fabric of your cosmic self.

For example:

A Mercury in Aquarius in the 9th house may indicate a communicative style that thrives on innovative ideas, especially in the realm of higher education or philosophy.

Venus in Leo in the 5th house may suggest a flair for romance, creativity, and a penchant for being in the spotlight when it comes to matters of the heart.

Practice Makes Profound

As you embark on your journey of interpreting birth charts, remember that mastery comes with practice. Don't hesitate to experiment with various narratives and make bold observations. Virtual communities, like the Constellation Club, provide valuable platforms for seeking feedback and sharing insights, especially when you're just starting out.

Trust the Cosmic Timing

Above all, embrace the mystical axiom that "you will know what you need to know when you need to know it." Trust the unfolding process of understanding astrology, your birth chart, and the cosmic wisdom it holds. Your cosmic self-revelation will occur precisely when it's meant to, unveiling the profound truths of your unique celestial blueprint.

other aspects of your stellar self

The Ascendant, often referred to as the Rising Sign, is one of the most critical components of a birth chart. It represents the zodiac sign that was rising on the eastern horizon at the time of your birth. Here's what it signifies:

- Outer Persona: The Ascendant represents the mask you wear when you interact with the world. It's your outward appearance, how you present yourself to others, and your first impression on people.

- Physical Appearance: While not an exact indicator of your physical appearance, the Ascendant can provide insights into your general demeanor, body language, and style.
- Life Path: It can offer clues about your life path and the areas of life where you'll take the initiative. It's like the "front door" to your personality.
- First House Ruler: The zodiac sign of your Ascendant also rules your first house. The planets located in this house and their aspects can provide additional details about your self-image and personal identity.
- Modifies Sun Sign: Your Ascendant can modify some of the traits associated with your Sun sign. For example, if you're a Cancer Sun with a Leo Ascendant, you might exhibit more extroverted and confident qualities than a typical Cancer.

Lunar Nodes (North Node and South Node):

The Lunar Nodes, often referred to as the North Node and South Node, represent points where the Moon's orbit intersects with the ecliptic (the apparent path of the Sun through the zodiac). They are not actual celestial bodies but mathematical points, and they hold significant karmic and evolutionary insights:

- North Node (Rahu): The North Node represents your soul's path of growth and evolution in this lifetime. It points to qualities, experiences, and behaviors you need to develop and embrace for personal and spiritual growth. It often indicates areas where you may face challenges or feel uncomfortable, but they are essential for your progress.

- South Node (Ketu): The South Node represents your past experiences and tendencies from previous lifetimes. While it can signify talents and skills you bring with you into this life, it can also represent patterns and behaviors that may hold you back if overindulged. It's considered your comfort zone but can hinder your growth if relied upon excessively.
- Sign and House Placement: The signs and houses where your North Node and South Node are located provide more specific information about the areas of life where these energies play out. The sign of your North Node often points to qualities you need to develop, while the South Node's sign indicates where you have natural abilities.
- Aspects: The aspects (angular relationships) between the Lunar Nodes and other planets in your chart can provide further insights into how these karmic energies interact with your personality and life circumstances.
- Understanding the Ascendant and Lunar Nodes in your birth chart can deepen your self-awareness and offer guidance for personal growth and life's journey. Keep in mind that while astrology can provide valuable insights, it's essential to use this knowledge as a tool for self-improvement and not as a deterministic or fatalistic view of life.

Planet schemes

In astrology, a planet scheme, often referred to as a "planetary pattern" or "planet distribution," is a specific arrangement of planets within the birth chart wheel. These schemes provide valuable insights into an individual's personality, strengths, and challenges. Here's an explanation of some common planet schemes you might encounter in an astrological birth chart:

Grand Trine

Description: A grand trine forms when three planets are evenly spaced (about 120 degrees apart) around the birth chart wheel, creating an equilateral triangle.

Interpretation: Grand trines are considered harmonious configurations, often associated with natural talents and ease in the areas represented by the involved elements (e.g., water signs for emotional intelligence). However, they can also indicate a tendency to become complacent or overly self-assured.

T-Square

Description: A T-square involves three planets forming a right triangle within the birth chart. Two planets oppose each other (180 degrees apart), and a third planet squares (forms a 90-degree angle with) both of them.

Interpretation: T-squares represent areas of tension, challenge, and growth in an individual's life. The opposition creates a push-pull dynamic, while the square aspect intensifies the conflict. T-squares can indicate areas where the person must work to find balance and resolution.

Yod (Finger of God)

Description: A yod is a rare aspect pattern involving three planets. Two planets sextile each other (60 degrees apart), and both quincunx (150 degrees) a third planet.

Interpretation: Yods are often seen as indicators of destiny or a significant mission in an individual's life. The planet at the apex of the yod represents a focal point of learning and spiritual growth. Yods suggest a need to integrate seemingly unrelated areas of life and make unique contributions.

Kite

Description: A kite is an extension of the grand trine pattern. It includes a fourth planet that opposes one of the planets in the grand trine and sextiles the other two.

Interpretation: Kites combine the harmonious energy of the grand trine with the potential for personal growth and challenge indicated by the opposition. They can signify opportunities for individuals to express their talents and navigate life's complexities.

Bucket

Description: A bucket pattern occurs when all planets are clustered within half of the birth chart, leaving one empty half devoid of planets.

Interpretation: The planet that stands alone in the empty half becomes the "handle" of the bucket and carries significant emphasis. It represents a focal point for the individual's life path and purpose. The bucket pattern suggests that the person's energy is directed toward the qualities and themes of the "handle" planet.

See-Saw

Description: In a see-saw pattern, planets are distributed relatively evenly on either side of the chart, with an axis of opposition running through the middle.

Interpretation: See-saw patterns suggest a constant balancing act between opposing forces or desires. The individual may experience shifts between different areas of life or qualities, seeking equilibrium and resolution.

Understanding these planet schemes within a birth chart can provide deeper insights into an individual's unique character, life challenges, and potential strengths. Astrologers analyze these patterns to offer more nuanced and accurate readings, guiding individuals toward self-awareness and personal growth.

CHAPTER 7
UNVEIL YESTERDAY,
TODAY TOMORROW

W E'VE UNRAVELED THE COSMIC CODE ENCODED

IN YOUR BIRTH CHART. NOW, let's delve into a fascinating aspect of astrology: the ability to unveil not only your past and present but also catch a glimpse of what the future might hold. This is achieved by marrying the birth chart with the positions of the stars today and in the days to come.

Charting the Stars Today

The birth chart serves as your cosmic fingerprint, a snapshot of the celestial energies at the moment of your birth. But what about today? How can you understand the ongoing cosmic dance of the planets and their influence on your life right now?

This is where transit astrology comes into play. Transits involve the current positions of the planets in the sky and their relationship to the planets in your birth chart. By superimposing these transiting planets onto your natal chart, you gain valuable insights into how the cosmic energies are currently affecting you.

Yesterday, Today, Tomorrow
Understanding Transits

Yesterday: Retroactive Insights

By analyzing past transits, you can gain retrospective insights into significant life events and personal growth. Past transits reveal the cosmic backdrop against which your life unfolded. For example, a major life change during a Saturn transit might have involved lessons in discipline and responsibility.

Today: Navigating the Present

Current transits offer a real-time view of the celestial influences shaping your daily life. For instance, a Mercury transit to your natal Venus might enhance communication in your relationships or bring opportunities for creative expression. Understanding these influences empowers you to make informed decisions and navigate your life more consciously.

Tomorrow: Cosmic Previews

Looking ahead to future transits, you can prepare for potential themes and opportunities. Perhaps a Jupiter transit to your natal Sun hints at a period of growth and expansion in your personal life or career. Anticipating these cosmic previews allows you to align your intentions and actions with the cosmic flow.

The Need for Speed: Understanding Planet Velocity in Astrology

In astrology, a transit is the movement of a planet across the zodiac from its position at the time of your birth. Transits can be used to predict changes and developments in your life.

The planets move at different speeds, so the length of a transit can vary. Some transits are very short, lasting only a few days or weeks. Others can last for months or even years.

the speed at which planets move across the heavens holds profound significance. Planet velocity plays a pivotal role in determining the depth and nature of their influence on your birth chart and the transits that shape your life's journey. Let's unravel the importance of planet velocity in the realm of astrology.

In astrology, planets are categorized into two broad groups based on their velocity: speedy planets and slow planets. Speedy planets, including Mercury, Venus, and Mars, are swift-footed travelers through the zodiac. They are often referred to as personal planets because their movements are relatively rapid, and their effects are more closely tied to individual experiences.

On the other hand, slow planets, such as Jupiter, Saturn, Uranus, Neptune, and Pluto, are the cosmic tortoises of the celestial race. They move at a glacial pace, taking years or even decades to traverse a single zodiac sign. These planets are known as generational planets because their transits are shared by entire generations and have a broader societal impact.

When delving into the realm of transits, astrologers assign greater significance to the impact of slower planets. Why? The effects of slow-moving planets are akin to the tides of the ocean—gradual, deep-reaching, and transformative over time. These transits shape collective experiences and societal shifts, leaving an indelible mark on history.

While speedy planets may not have the same long-lasting impact as their slower counterparts, they serve as celestial switches in the intricate astral machinery. Their swift movements trigger and activate more complex configurations in your birth chart. These planetary triggers set the stage for events and experiences, often marking key moments in your life.

In essence, planet velocity in astrology is a dynamic interplay between the rapid and the gradual, the personal and the collective, and the immediate and the enduring. Understanding the unique role of both speedy and slow planets enriches our comprehension of the cosmic symphony that shapes our lives, offering valuable insights into our past, present, and future.

Planet transit meaning

let's delve into the meanings of planet transits for each of the major celestial players in astrology:

Sun Transit: When the Sun transits a specific sign in your birth chart, it illuminates that area of your life. It's a time for self-expression, vitality, and focusing on personal goals. However, it can also highlight your ego and identity issues.

Moon Transit: Lunar transits influence your emotional state and instincts. As the Moon moves through different signs, it can impact your mood, reactions, and intuition. It's a key player in your day-to-day emotional experiences.

Mercury Transit: Mercury's transits affect communication, thinking, and intellectual pursuits. When Mercury transits a sign, it's an excellent time for mental clarity, learning, and expressing your thoughts effectively.

Venus Transit: Venus governs love, relationships, beauty, and aesthetics. Its transits can bring romantic opportunities, social harmony, and a desire for indulgence. However, they can also highlight issues related to self-worth and materialism.

Mars Transit: Mars is the planet of action, energy, and assertiveness. Its transits can inspire courage, ambition, and the drive to pursue your goals. On the flip side, they can also lead to impulsiveness and conflicts.

Jupiter Transit: Jupiter represents expansion, growth, and opportunities. Its transits often bring luck, optimism, and a sense of abundance. They're associated with personal and spiritual development, as well as learning experiences.

Saturn Transit: Saturn's transits are about discipline, responsibility, and structure. They can be challenging, as they may bring obstacles and limitations. However, they also provide opportunities for personal growth, maturity, and long-term success.

Uranus Transit: Uranus is the planet of change, innovation, and unpredictability. Its transits can shake up your life, bringing sudden insights, breakthroughs, and a desire for freedom. They're often associated with unexpected events.

Neptune Transit: Neptune represents dreams, intuition, and spirituality. Its transits can inspire creativity, imagination, and a longing for deeper meaning. They can also create confusion, illusion, and a need to address issues related to escapism.

Pluto Transit: Pluto is associated with transformation, power, and regeneration. Its transits can lead to profound inner and outer changes, often involving letting go of the old to make way for the new. They can be intense and transformative.

These planetary transits interact with the positions of planets in your birth chart, creating a unique cosmic tapestry of influences. Astrologers examine these transits to gain insights into life's opportunities, challenges, and the timing of significant events. Keep in mind that the specific effects of a transit depend on the planets involved, the signs they're transiting, and their aspects to other planets in your chart.

CONCLUSION

YOUR PATH START NOW

A S WE REACH THE CULMINATION OF THIS

CELESTIAL VOYAGE through the world of astrology, it's time to reflect on the path you've traveled and the knowledge you've gained. We embarked on this journey to unravel the mysteries of the stars, to understand the impact of astrology on our lives, and to discover the transformative power it holds.

In Chapter 1, we delved into the challenges of living a life without astrology. We explored the void it leaves, the missed opportunities for self-awareness, and the fear of the unknown that often accompanies it.

Chapter 2 illuminated the potential for personal transformation. By becoming a "Starchild," you learned how astrology can unlock your inner power, providing insights into your true self and your unique path in life.

Chapter 3 allowed us to dive deeper into the history and essence of astrology. You unveiled the rich story of this ancient art and how it has evolved to become a timeless guide for understanding the cosmos.

In Chapter 4, we ventured into the foundational aspects of astrology. You grasped the significance of planets, zodiac signs, and houses, building the knowledge required to decipher your birth chart.

Chapter 5 emphasized the critical role of the natal chart in setting the stars in motion. With the birth chart as our compass, we connected the dots between planets, signs, and houses, revealing the intricate tapestry of your life.

Chapter 6 introduced the fascinating world of transits, the key to understanding the past, present, and future. You explored how planetary movements influence your life, offering insights into your experiences and challenges.

Now, in this concluding chapter, your journey into the world of astrology has reached its beginning. Armed with the wisdom gained from these chapters, you stand at the threshold of a new phase of life—one infused with self-awareness, empowerment, and cosmic wonder.

Your path starts now. Armed with the insights of astrology, you are better equipped to navigate life's twists and turns. You have the tools to unlock your potential, embrace change, and connect with the rhythm of the universe

As you continue your exploration of astrology, remember that this ancient art is not just about the stars above but about the stars within you. Your unique birth chart is a roadmap to self-discovery, a guide to making conscious choices, and a reminder that you are an integral part of the cosmic dance.

Your journey through the cosmos has only just begun. May the stars forever light your path as you embark on a life filled with purpose, meaning, and boundless cosmic wonder. The universe awaits your next steps, and your destiny is in your hands. Your path starts now, and it's a journey of self-discovery, growth, and infinite possibilities.

And now ?

As you embark on your journey into the world of astrology, it's essential to remember that knowledge gains its true power through application. The wisdom you've acquired in these chapters is not meant to remain dormant but to be actively integrated into your life.

To facilitate this integration and to help you put theory into practice, I've included a series of example birth charts in the following pages. These charts will serve as valuable tools for you to apply the knowledge you've acquired throughout this book.

In each example, you'll have the opportunity to explore the nuances of different birth charts, decipher the positions of planets, signs, and houses, and gain a deeper understanding of the individuals behind these charts. By analyzing these examples, you'll learn to connect the celestial dots, make astrological interpretations, and uncover the unique stories woven within each birth chart.

Remember that astrology is both an art and a science, and like any skill, it grows stronger with practice. As you delve into these example charts, allow your intuition to guide you. Trust in your ability to decode the cosmic messages hidden within the birth chart, and don't be afraid to experiment with different interpretations.

Your journey into astrology is a dynamic, ever-evolving process. Just as the stars continue their celestial dance, so too will your understanding of the cosmos deepen with time and experience. So, seize this opportunity to apply your newfound knowledge, embrace the mysteries of the universe, and let the stars be your guiding light.

May your exploration of astrology be filled with insight, wonder, and a sense of cosmic connection. Your journey begins now, and the universe eagerly awaits your discoveries.

Study Natal Chart

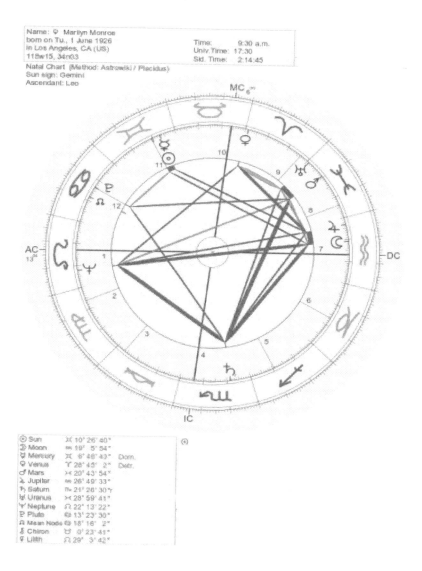

Name: ♀ Marilyn Monroe
born on Tu., 1 June 1926
in Los Angeles, CA (US)
118w15, 34n03

Time: 9:30 a.m.
Univ. Time: 17:30
Std. Time: 2:14:45

Natal Chart (Method: Astrowiki / Placidus)
Sun sign: Gemini
Ascendant: Leo

☉ Sun	♓ 10° 26' 40"	
☽ Moon	♒ 19° 5' 54"	
☿ Mercury	♓ 6° 48' 43"	Dom.
♀ Venus	♈ 28° 45' 2"	Detr.
♂ Mars	♓ 20° 43' 54"	
♃ Jupiter	♒ 26° 49' 33"	
♄ Saturn	♏ 21° 28' 30" ℞	
♅ Uranus	♓ 28° 59' 41"	
♆ Neptune	♌ 22° 13' 22"	
♇ Pluto	♋ 13° 23' 30"	
☊ Mean Node	♋ 18° 16' 2"	
⚷ Chiron	♉ 0° 23' 41"	
⚸ Lilith	♌ 29° 3' 42"	

Marilyn Monroe's astrological chart paints an intriguing picture of her life. With Cancer as her ascendant and Capricorn as her Moon sign, she possessed a unique blend of qualities that defined her captivating persona. The Moon, her personal planet, graced her 7th house, which governs public image. This placement hinted at her extraordinary allure, characterized by her enchanting eyes, a beguiling smile, an attractive countenance, and a physique imbued with both sensuality and intellectual prowess. These attributes were perfectly suited for her illustrious career as a dancer, model, and film star.

Conversely, the influence of Cancer ascendant, governed by intense emotions, cast a shadow over her personal life. Her private affairs were marked by turbulence but were undeniably captivating to the public eye. Saturn, the ruler of the 7th house associated with partnerships and marriage, was positioned in the 4th house, exalted in Venus. This configuration bestowed upon her immense public attention and material wealth, yet it withheld marital bliss. The 7th house's lord, Saturn, also received the unsettling aspect of Rahu, positioned in the 12th house. Additionally, Venus, symbolizing love and marriage, was afflicted by Saturn and Rahu, contributing to the troubles in her married life, culminating in divorce in 1946. Explore the intricacies of your own love story through our marriage astrology report.

A closer examination of her horoscope reveals that Saturn in the 4th house, Moon in the 7th house, and Venus in the 10th house signify her peak career achievements in 1949 when she posed for a nude calendar, catapulting her into the spotlight. Venus connected her to the realms of glamour, show business, and beauty, while the Moon in the 7th house ensured her prominence. Despite criticisms and challenges, she found happiness in her fame, owing to her boldness.

Venturing into the astrological realm of Marilyn Monroe's horoscope, we witness the intertwined narratives of fame and adversity that continue to resonate today.

Saturn's placement in the 4th house and the Moon in the 7th house, along with Venus in the 10th house, endowed Cancer ascendants like her with creative talents but often a troubled upbringing. They are extraordinarily sensitive individuals, oscillating between intellectual brilliance and emotional intensity, which can lead to tendencies toward addiction, such as alcohol or drugs.

Mars, the ruler of the 5th house related to creativity, talent, and love, resided in the 8th house, indicating obstacles and disruptions in her life. This placement negatively impacted her sexual orientation, fostering short-lived, often disappointing affairs, both physically and emotionally.

Jupiter, governing the 6th house (enemies, debt, and disease), in the 8th house of sexual orientation, signaled her excessive indulgence in sexual activities. Marilyn's Cancer ascendant, coupled with the influences of Jupiter, Mars, and Ketu, drove her into numerous sexual involvements and the infamous nude calendar scandal, bestowing fame but eroding her peace.

Her ascendant lord, the Moon, occupying the 7th house of marriage, heightened her sensitivity in relationships, resulting in multiple marriages that vacillated between joy and agony, with none proving successful.

Meanwhile, Jupiter and Mars in the 8th house contributed to her fame and wealth but posed significant challenges to her personal life.

Sun and Mercury, located in the 11th house of gains, did not exert a dominant influence, yielding a relatively modest impact on her overall reputation and financial success.

Rahu in the 12th house symbolized her disillusionment in matters of intimacy, perpetuating her unhappiness in marriage and ultimately leading to divorce.

Transits charts

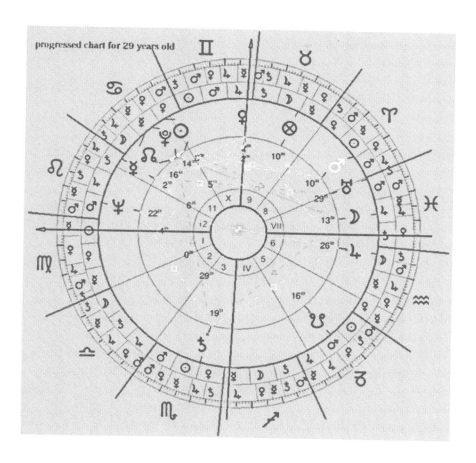

progressed chart for 29 years old

In 1955, Marilyn Monroe found herself still in the Sun sub-period within a 13-year Mercury period. The Sun held a significant position in her astrological chart, closely aligned with Mercury. This alignment hinted at a period of considerable importance, particularly concerning her self-image (as the Sun ruled her natal chart) and how she communicated through it. During this time, Marilyn made a memorable impact in the iconic scene where she wore a white dress that flowed gracefully, almost like poetry. Her hands, symbolizing her Gemini nature, discreetly covered her private parts, conveying a message like, "I can exude sensuality without revealing everything," or so we might imagine. Notably, her natal Sun and Mercury were both in Gemini, reinforcing this theme of communication and self-expression.

Now, let's turn our attention to Marilyn's progressed chart for 1955. In this chart, we witness the formation of a powerful grand trine configuration. This alignment was activated by the presence of the progressed Moon in her 7th house, associated with the public image and relationships. The other two points of this celestial triangle involved Pluto in the 11th house, representing large corporations like Fox Studios, and progressed Saturn, signifying her career.

This astrological arrangement suggests that during this time, Marilyn's public image and relationships played a pivotal role in her life. Her connection to a major corporation, possibly symbolized by Fox Studios, and the influence of her career (Saturn) converged harmoniously under the auspices of this grand trine. It was a moment when her star power was in full bloom, and her public persona was closely aligned with her career aspirations. This period likely marked a significant phase in her life, where she achieved a remarkable balance between her personal image, her interactions with the public, and her professional ambitions.

these 2 examples are an indicative guide to help you develop
your personal interpretative technique.

remember that you need to gain experience analysing your
charts to become an astrology expert!

Have a good journey!

ABOUTH

THE AUTHOR

Giovanni da Rupecisa has always been drawn to the mystical and esoteric realms from a young age. Growing up, the author was no stranger to the world of magic and spirituality. Early encounters with astrology, tarot cards, and the study of ancient mysteries ignited a lifelong fascination with the unseen forces that shape our existence.

Fifteen years ago, life took an unexpected turn, throwing challenges and tribulations in Giovanni's path. These trials became the catalyst for a profound awakening. The author found himself at a crossroads, compelled to explore the depths of spirituality and seek answers to life's most profound questions.

This pivotal moment marked the beginning of Giovanni's dedicated journey into the world of esoteric wisdom. In the vast universe of spiritual knowledge, he discovered astrology as a powerful and illuminating tool. It became the guiding star on his quest for self-discovery and understanding.

It was during these moments of soul-searching that Giovanni's connection to the mystical arts deepened. He found solace in the study of astrology, a profound tool that helped him navigate life's challenges and find purpose in the cosmic dance of the stars. The author's own journey of self-discovery through astrology inspired the creation of "Astrology for Beginners: Stars Hold the Key of Your Life Path."

In this book, Giovanni da Rupecisa shares not only his knowledge of astrology but also his personal experience of how this ancient wisdom has transformed his life. With a genuine passion for helping others unlock the potential of their own life paths, the author invites readers to embark on a transformative journey through the cosmos.

Today, Giovanni da Rupecisa is recognized as a leading authority on esoterics in Europe and Italy. He has become a revered teacher and mentor, sharing his wealth of knowledge with eager students around the world. Through his visionary editorial project, "Templum Dianae", thousands of students, more than 20,000 each month, gather to explore the mysteries of astrology, tarot, and various facets of the esoteric arts.

In "Astrology for Beginners: Stars Hold the Key of Your Life Path," Giovanni's passion for spiritual exploration and his commitment to empowering others shine brightly. This book is a testament to his profound journey of self-discovery and the transformative power of astrology. Join Giovanni as he invites you to unlock the secrets of the stars, embark on your own voyage of self-awareness, and discover the boundless potential that resides within you. "Astrology for Beginners" is not just a book; it's an initiation into the magical world of cosmic wisdom, guided by an author who has dedicated his life to illuminating the path for others.

**Teaching Materials
included**

Scan this code to get
your Video Course included in the book, an introduction to the
world of the occult and the paranormal

Or follow this link:

https://templumdianae.co/the-witchy-course/

This Material will give you access to Exclusive training materials
to improve in your path !

Printed in Great Britain
by Amazon

27172007R00067